W9-BQX-847

Walking – The Pleasure Exercise

Walking –
The Pleasure Exercise

A 60-Day Walking Program for Fitness and Health

by Mort Malkin

 Rodale Press, Emmaus, Pa.

Copyright © 1986 by Mort Malkin

All rights reserved. No part of this publication may be reproduced or transmitted in any form or by any means, electronic or mechanical, including photocopy, recording, or any information storage and retrieval system, without the written permission of the publisher.

Printed in the United States of America on recycled paper containing a high percentage of de-inked fiber.

Book design and layout by Denise Mirabello

Library of Congress Cataloging in Publication Data

Malkin, Mort.
  Walking: the pleasure exercise.

    Bibliography: p.
    Includes index.
    1. Physical fitness.   2. Walking.   I. Title.
GV481.M29   1986   796.5′1   85-28263
ISBN 0-87857-614-2   hardcover
ISBN 0-87857-608-8   paperback

  4   6   8   10   9   7   5   hardcover
  4   6   8   10   9   7   5   paperback

Notice

This book is intended as a reference volume only, not as a medical manual or guide to self-treatment. Keep in mind that exercise and nutritional needs vary from person to person, depending on age, sex, and health status. Before engaging in a strenuous exercise program, it is important for you to consult your physician.

Contents

Chapter 1

Health: A Step in the Right Direction

The Walking Program—Level One

How do you take care of your health? Do you nurture it by providing your body with the proper nutrition? If you do, you know that you must eat a wide variety of wholesome foods, such as fresh fruits and vegetables, lean meats, and whole grains.

Complete health, though, is more than just providing high-quality fuel for the body's engine. The *running* of that living engine is also vital. Your muscles and bones and your heart and lungs must be able to do their work without creaking and groaning. This second side of health is fitness. Your body needs both fitness and nutrition to keep its tissues and organs functioning smoothly. It needs the complete health that confers toughness and resistance against illness.

The idea of fitness for health dates back to the ancient Greeks, who celebrated the healthy, beautiful body.

Since that time, many individuals and even entire cultures used physical activity to gain fitness and health. In the early 1900s, "physical culture"—sound-mind-in-a-sound-body—was promoted for health and longevity. In the 1970s, running became the favored road to fitness, and it still is.

Now, research has confirmed what the fitness folks have always believed: exercise may help to protect you from a heart attack, especially a fatal heart attack; and exercise may increase your life span.

These findings came from several studies conducted across the nation, involving many thousands of subjects. The studies were well designed and their conclusions rest on firm ground. Even the medical profession at large accepts the work as valid.

Beyond the say-so of the medicine men and the physical activists, it makes good common sense that if the body is mostly

1

muscle and bone, it was meant to move about. In fact, our evolutionary ancestors were up and about much of the time. They had to forage for edible roots, fruit, and berries. They went on hunting expeditions. They migrated with climate changes, and they traveled great distances when new food sources were needed. Those who had stamina were more likely to survive and pass their traits on to their children. Today, we are physiologically much the same as our ancestors who were hunters and gatherers. We are, as they were, healthiest when active.

Nowadays, we have many more physical activities to choose from than our ancestors had in prehistoric times. The question is, "What exercise is best?" The answer depends on whom you ask.

The runners say, "Run for your life." The cyclists push pedaling. The skiers say ski, the rowers row, the swimmers swim. Along with the dozens of sports, performed on land, in the air, and in/on water, snow, or ice, there are high-test combinations: biathlon, triathlon, pentathlon, and decathlon. It is enough to confuse the wise and to intimidate the brave.

You can resolve all the confusion and choosing in one deft stroke: use *walking* as your exercise. Walking uses the muscles of the legs and hips, and the arm swing gives the shoulders and arms

Decisions, decisions, decisions!

a workout. You can easily make walking into a full-scale exercise for fitness.

You will not have to learn new skills; you already know how to put one foot in front of the other to walk from point A to point B. All you need is a little instruction to gain efficiency and a touch of grace, and that will do the trick.

You will not be taking chances with injury. Let the runners worry about shin splints and hamstring tears. Let the weight lifters worry about back injuries. Walking is virtually risk-free. I will show you how to turn walking into an exercise for health and longevity.

Health: A Small Investment Pays Large Dividends

If you are able to walk for 10 continuous minutes—5 minutes one way and 5 minutes back—you can start my walking program. In the beginning, it does not matter how fast or slow you are. It does not matter whether you look like an Olympian doing a workout for form or a duck with fallen arches. All you need is the desire to improve your health.

I will guide you in sharpening your walking ability, and I will show you how a walk can be a workout. You will have a schedule to follow, and I will tell you what to expect from your body along the way.

If you are diligent, you will progress to complete fitness in four easy stages. In two weeks you will reach Level One and feel the satisfaction of accomplishment that comes with making a good beginning. The second two weeks will take you to Level Two and the third two weeks to Level Three. Each week will bring further stamina, strength, and confidence. The last two weeks will bring you to your goal: Level Four.

When you reach Level Four, the fitness plateau, you will have a sense of assurance about your walking. You will be able to walk farther and faster than people who are many years younger—in fact, you'll wear them out. After all, you are fit and they are not.

When I first began to walk for exercise it was at the suggestion of an older friend who walked regularly five times a week. Dave was 64 years old and I was 42 when we began to walk together on Sunday mornings. We would meet at a neighborhood park, and for the first mile and a half (once around the park), I was just about able to keep up with him. Then, I gradually fell behind, and at 3 miles I was ready to call it a day. Dave, who had passed the 3-mile mark fully 3 minutes before, kept on going to complete 4½ miles.

Choosing Shoes

For serious walking, you should have the kind of shoes with thick cushion soles and heels made of a crepe material. Try them on for proper fit, comfort, and the feeling of good support. The sneakers made for general knocking around are not substantial enough, or supportive enough, for a true walking program. Of course, high heels and many of the more bizarre shoe styles are out of the question.

Here's how to shop for shoes:

- Hold the heel of the shoe in one hand and try to bend up the front end; it should be easy to do.

- Check for a decent arch support to avoid stressing the inside of the foot as you walk.

- Check for a padded lining in the part of the shoe that encases the heel, since that will help to prevent irritation.

- Look for a "bouncy" type of crepe material for the sole of the shoe.

- The best fit comes in a shoe that allows ½ to ¾ inch between the longest toe and the front of the shoe.

- The covering material for the shoe should "breathe." Natural substances, rather than synthetics, are best.

And so it went almost every Sunday for a year. Occasionally I would do an exercise walk during the week, but mostly it was only on Sunday with Dave.

The following year, my life was punctuated by tragedy and near tragedy among family, friends, and colleagues—seven heart attacks in all. I decided that I'd better set aside time to become more than just a weekend warrior. Workouts once a week would not hold off the coronary gremlins. I began to walk two or three times on weekdays and continued to meet Dave on Sundays. Strength and endurance came fast, and within two months I was able to keep up with him for the full distance.

It does not take long to become fit once you make a commitment to your health. You must *walk for exercise* three to four times a week. Only then will your body know you are serious about your workouts. At once or twice a week your metabolism will regard you as a dilettante and will humor you at best. The key is to make walking a regular routine.

There is, of course, more to walking for fitness than merely going out for a walk three or four times a week. But let us take one step at a time and begin with the requirement of frequency. Three to four times a week—approximately every other day—will establish the proper cycle of exercise and rest. The other facets of health walking—distance, intensity, and form—will come one by one in their own time.

Nor should you think of any walking you do on your job as proper walking for fitness. I can't think of anyone whose work involves the type of walking that leads to fitness: not door to door salesmen, not letter carriers, not secretaries whose bosses ask for this file or that 50 times a day. Walking for health is important enough and its requirements exacting enough that it should be an independent activity done for its own sake. Time should be set aside for health walking and counted as high priority time. After all, your health is surely among your highest priorities.

Benefits without Risk

The benefits of walking for fitness are many and varied. The metabolic changes that come about with fitness will make you lean and trim without extreme dieting, will lower your blood pressure if it is on the high side, and will strengthen the bone structure of your body. Walking will not only rejuvenate your body, it will be a mental tonic as well. Fitness will cause actual biochemical changes that will improve carbohydrate and fat metabolism and reduce anxiety and depression

There are more than a dozen specific beneficial health changes that result from the exercise of walking. Considering the small investment, the dividends are truly impressive.

Among the many reasons why walking yields health are two basic ones: it is exercise and it is moderate.

Because walking is moderate exercise, it is suitable for almost everyone: the young and old, the weak and strong, the graceful and clumsy. Few doctors would object to walking as an exercise, especially if the walking program begins with an easy 10-minute walk every other day, as this one does. Even those physicians whose basic philosophy is, "Why wear yourself out?" will agree to it.

Let your doctor know that you are going to start my walking program and that you will continue to make brisk walking a way of life. If you are overdue for a complete physical examination, now is a good time to have that done.

The Walking Program: The First Easy Step

Level One is as simple as it is easy.

Week One:
Walk 10 minutes every other day.

Notes for Week One:

- Your exercise walk must be done for itself and may not be included in another activity such as walking to the supermarket or walking from the bus to your office.

- The 10 minutes should be continuous. Do not stop at a neighbor's house for tea in the middle of your workout. Your body will know you are not dedicated.

- If you miss a day, it is not critical. Just walk the following day (normally an off day). Of course, this grace day rule should not become a habit and should not be carried to an extreme. For example, you should not try to do three workouts on a weekend and count that as exercise for the week.

The prescription for Week One is so simple that you shouldn't try to find a way around it.

Week Two:
Walk 15 minutes every other day.

Notes for Week Two:

- Week Two must follow Week One without interruption.

- The notes for Week One apply to Week Two.

- You may start to walk a bit briskly and should keep good posture as you stride along. Walk as if you are proud of your efforts.

When you have completed the first two weeks of the Program, you will be ready for Level Two. You won't be completely fit yet, but you will have taken the most difficult step toward that goal—the first step.

Chapter 2

Taking Exercise in Stride

Warming Up to Level Two

You are now a serious student of walking. Two weeks of consistent walking for exercise and you are no longer a dilettante.

Has it seemed too easy? Well, I suppose that two weeks of 10- and 15-minute gentle workouts are not enough to prepare you for the Olympics, but you have earned the strength, endurance, and self-confidence needed to enter the second level of my Walking Program.

Your muscles are now nicely toned, and you are not out of breath after walking twice around the block. There is even a little spring in your stride. These gains in fitness will be tested in the next two weeks.

The first week of Level Two will call for workouts of 22 minutes; the second week, 33 minutes. If you walk at a fair pace you will cover well over a mile in 22 minutes. Thirty-three minutes will bring you close to 2 miles. These are serious distances, and you must not treat such workouts in a casual way.

Prepare Yourself before You Exercise

Vigorous exercise, whatever the sport, can cause soreness and stiffness if you are unprepared or if the exercise is too sudden, severe, prolonged, or even too frequent. Two or three of these negative influences can gang up on you to cause actual injury. You can prevent all pain and suffering if you go about your exercise properly and patiently. The Walking Program you have started is based on proven precepts of sports medicine concerning the workings of the cardiovascular system, the ins and outs of carbohydrate and fat metabolism, aerobic and anaerobic muscle function, and many other of the body's ways of doing business. Yet, the program is so easy to follow that you will not have to give the

7

arteries or the muscle cells of your legs and heart a second thought.

You may be surprised to know that you are already following three important principles of biomechanical safekeeping. First, you have selected walking, the safe sport, for physical fitness. Second, you are exercising no more than every other day, which gives your musculoskeletal system a good 48 hours for rest and recuperation. Third, you are building stamina in a gradual fashion, increasing your distance by just 50 percent each week.

And now there are other things to do.

Warming Up

Warming up raises the temperature of the body's tissues, and this helps to achieve several benefits.

- You are less likely to pull muscles or tear tendons.

- Muscle viscosity is reduced, allowing for easier and faster contraction of the muscles.

- Blood supply to the working muscles is increased.

- Oxygen is more easily released from the hemoglobin of the red blood cells.

- The blood flow to the heart itself via the coronary arteries responds faster and to a greater maximum whenever the heart must meet the demands of sudden vigorous exercise.

You probably need no further convincing that warm-ups are necessary, but the results of one particular study were so dramatic they deserve special mention. R. James Barnard of the U.C.L.A. School of Medicine and Kinesiology studied a group of normal, healthy fire fighters. Each of the men was connected to an EKG monitor and then placed on a treadmill. They were asked to run at full speed for 10 seconds, starting from a standstill. Sixty percent of the subjects showed abnormal electrocardiographic changes. When the men warmed up before the full-speed run, few showed abnormal EKG changes, and those who did had milder deviations from normal.

It is a basic axiom of sports medicine that the human body reacts poorly to sudden change but can tolerate stress if the exposure is gradual. Your muscles need that little physiologic pep talk before any serious workout. It is a small concession to make. How do you warm up? You have these choices:

- Warm up the entire body with physical heat, a hot tub for example.

- Perform a series of calisthenics that provides a general muscular warm-up.

- Do a specific muscular warm-up by doing the workout exercise itself at half to three-quarters pace.

All three types of warm-ups will work for exercise walking, but the specific muscular warm-up is best. It warms up the very muscles, tendons, and ligaments that will be contracting and relaxing at the rate of twice a second (perhaps faster) for a full 22 or 33 minutes per workout. And those muscles will have to contract under a work load of your body's full weight. The specific muscular warm-up also gives you a good neuromuscular rehearsal of the coordination and balance that will be required in your workout. You will be able to practice the form you will use and the continuous rhythm you should feel.

Start your warm-up with a couple of minutes of gentle strolling, and follow with 5 minutes of more purposeful walking. You will then be prepared for a brisk pace in your actual workout. It is that simple. Walking is the best warm-up for walking.

Form

Now that you know about warming up, you are almost ready for Level Two of my Walking Program. There is just one last precaution: you must avoid getting into any bad habits in your walking form.

In the first week of Level Two you will be walking for 22 minutes without stopping. That translates to approximately 2,000 strides. Such four-figure repetition will ingrain your walking habits, whether good or bad. Now is the time to develop good ones.

Why bother about form at all? It is fitness we're after. And fitness is the product of frequency times distance times intensity of exercise.

Yes, that is all true. But the program's goal is more than fitness; it is fitness without injury. By using large muscles for power at a fraction of full effort rather than using small muscles at close to peak effort, there will be less risk of injury. Good form looks effortless because it is large muscle work at a fraction of full power. Smooth coordination, another facet of form, also lessens risk of injury by avoiding sudden or awkward movements.

Aside from prevention of injury, grace is its own good reason to work on form. Why not be that person who walks into a room with such stature that others turn their heads to take note of your presence? My former assistant, Rina, was such a woman. She was tall and slim but had only average facial features. Yet, she attracted attention just walking from the office to her car. It was all in her carriage. Rina radiated class when she walked.

For some individuals, another reason to gain a smooth style of walking is pure, simple speed. To illustrate the direct relationship between form and speed, I'd like to tell you a story about two friends of mine, a pair of twins, Nina and Grace.

The two young women were especially conscious of their figures. They watched their diet and did a series of calisthenics every day. Grace, at her office, pinned up a magazine ad of a slim model in a bikini. I suggested to them that they take up walking as a metabolic exercise for slimness. They tried brisk walking, liked it, and kept it up. Within six months they became not only lean and sleek but also fast. They were fairly evenly matched, yet Nina always finished each workout a few steps ahead of Grace.

The twins decided to enter a road race as walkers and asked me for a little coaching. The next day only Grace was available to do a workout with me, and so the two of us went over to nearby Marine Park, where I worked on form and pace with her. We concentrated on achieving a fluid stride, especially the change from one foot to the next. We also tried for an easy arm swing. Grace showed immediate improvement in form and her speed seemed to increase as well. Two days later all three of us got together for a 3-mile workout in the park. Grace showed her new-found grace, whereas Nina's form was still effortful. Nina could not keep up with her sister, and at the end of 3 miles she was 200 yards behind. Form!

Improved Efficiency

Skeptics may argue that my personal observation of the twins is not a very scientific way to prove that efficient form results in greater speed. Let me cite a recent study that will add some weight to the form = speed equation. Douglas L. Conley, Ed.D., and his team of exercise physiologists at the Human Performance Laboratory at Arizona State University, Tempe, Arizona, studied Steve Scott, the United States record holder for the 1-mile run. They measured Scott's stamina (maximal aerobic capacity) and his running economy (percentage of maximal aerobic power used for a given pace). The results were then compared to the values reported ten years earlier for Jim Ryun, the previous American record holder in the mile.

The values for aerobic power for the two runners were virtually the same. That tells us that there was no difference in endurance between the two men. The values for running economy, however, were significantly different. At a measured pace Ryun used 62 percent of his aerobic power whereas Scott used only 57 percent of his. Scott's efficiency in running gave him the ability to break Ryun's record in the mile. Form equals efficiency, and efficiency equals speed.

Another study, this one using race-walkers as subjects, confirmed the Scott-Ryun comparison. Drs. James A. Hagberg and Edward F. Doyle, both of Washington University School of Medicine, St. Louis, Missouri, measured stamina and efficiency of motion in a group of competitive race-walkers. Then, the competitors' race performances were recorded. When race times were compared to stamina and efficiency results, the researchers found that efficiency was more closely related to winning races.

For those of you who don't have competitive urges, a faster walking pace with less effort is still worthwhile. It will enable you to breeze through Levels Two, Three, and Four of my Walking Program. There are other good reasons for speed—catching a bus a couple of blocks away or keeping up with the kids on a long hike.

Finally, walking with good form is a skill, and skills are valuable in their own right. Here, women have an advantage over men. Just as women do better at yoga and dance, so are they more natural walkers. Walking has attracted many women even when it is in the form of competitive race-walking, a sport of technique, stamina, and speed.

Don't despair, brothers—grace is not the sole preserve of women. Form is an equal opportunity element of walking for health and fitness.

Some Basics in Form

Now that you are convinced by all the good reasons for form in walking, let us work on a few pointers.

- Your posture in walking should be straight and upright. You should not lean forward, nor backward. You should feel that you are leading with your chest and pelvis equally. Your shoulders should be relaxed and not raised up as you swing your arms. How can you judge your own walking posture? If you feel some spirit is lifting you by the top of the head, then you are walking tall.

- Your feet should point straight ahead so they will be parallel to each other. They should not turn in pigeon-toed, and they should not turn out like duck feet.

- Your feet should fall on a straight line as you walk, neither crossing over nor stepping side to side. Ideally, the inside of the left foot should step on the same line as the inside of the right one. A white line on some deserted roadway is a good way to practice this concept.

- Your stride should be generous in length—not overstretched, not pinched too short.

- At the beginning of each stride, the heel touches the ground first. As you advance over that foot, your weight is transferred along its outer edge to the ball of the foot. Finally, at the end of the stride the large toe pushes off.

- There should be a smooth transition from stride to stride. Do not come down hard at each heel strike. Avoid a bouncing stride. Be graceful.

- The power for each stride should come from *pulling* during the first half of each stride more than *pushing off* in the last half. When you pull from the heel, you use the large muscles of the buttocks and the back of the thigh. The smaller calf muscles are pushing-off muscles and should be given proportionately less work to do. Use your hips for power and you will have a stride that looks strong, yet effort-free. Feel that you are reaching forward with the hip for each new stride. As one hip reaches forward, the other pushes the ground backward, and you're off in a cloud of amazement.

- Let your arms swing naturally to counterbalance your leg movement. Think more of your upper arm (from shoulder to elbow) acting as a pendulum. Do not give as much attention to the lower arm. If you wish, bend your arms 90 degrees at the elbow as race-walkers do. You will be able to move your arms faster to match a quick stride, and you will be able to concentrate more on your upper arm swing.

Correct Heel-and-Toe Walking

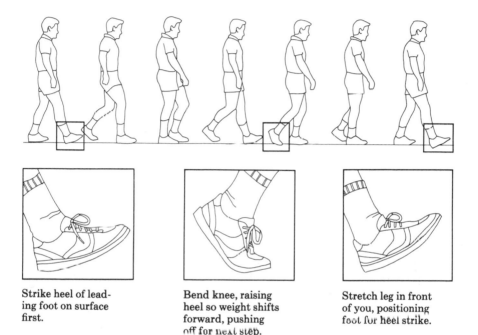

Strike heel of leading foot on surface first.

Bend knee, raising heel so weight shifts forward, pushing off for next step.

Stretch leg in front of you, positioning foot for heel strike.

It is not easy to think about all the facets of good form at the same moment. Good form takes concentration, analysis, and time. The individual elements can be added only one or two at a time, and you will have to review them every so often as you improve. Putting all the pieces together synchronously will need time, but elegant style is worth the patience.

There is another way to acquire good form. Instead of adding the pieces one by one, you might try learning by wholes. Watch people who walk well, those who walk effortlessly. Take in the entire motion and try to copy their form for smoothness. After a time you will be able to feel that your own motion is right. The following series of photographs illustrates the form. Of course, you will develop your own individual "style" within a good basic form.

Figure 1

Figure 2

Figure 3

A demonstration of the correct form for a brisk walking workout.

Learning by parts and learning by wholes need not be in conflict. You can use the two methods in synergy. As you gain the overall coordination and feel your form becoming more fluid, you can concentrate on one detail and then another. Perhaps the use of the hips for power would be a good early item to add to the overall rhythm.

There is still another way to improve form, but it can only be used after you have already attained some semblance of form. It is a supplement, not a substitute for the parts and wholes methods. Some athletes, mysteriously, have been able to improve while sitting around in an easy chair. Some tennis players and race-walkers use mental imagery to sharpen skills. My skier friend improves his balance and edge control over the summer months. By visualizing themselves performing the activity, they can feel the coordination, balance, and timing. This type of training won't give you any metabolic benefits, nor can you learn a new activity from ground zero. But once you know the basics you can polish your form with imaging. Such mental rehearsal can be added to your regular workout schedule. As your form becomes more fluid, you will more easily feel the movements to practice in your mind's eye.

The Walking Program

Level Two

Week One:
    Walk 22 minutes every other day. Keep a brisk pace.

Week Two:
    Walk 33 minutes every other day. Continue a brisk pace.

Notes for Level Two:

- Warm up by walking at an easy pace. First, mosey along for a couple of minutes. Then walk for 5 minutes at a deliberate pace but not as fast as your workout.

- The warm-up doesn't count toward the 22 or 33 minutes of your workout. Don't try to rationalize your way out of a few minutes of training time. Your body will know.

- Each workout must be continuous without extended pauses. Stopping to tie your shoelaces is not an extended pause. Stopping to have a conversation with a neighbor or a friend is an extended pause.

Do not try to rush fitness. Twenty-two minutes of brisk walking is a strong workout for the third week of the program, and three to four times a week will give your muscles enough work and enough rest. Do not be like my grandmother who was sure that three spoons of cod liver oil would make you three times as healthy as one spoonful would. Do not do 66-minute workouts just yet.

Be attentive to form. Try to be free and easy as you stride along. Use as little energy as you can for the speed you are walking. Walk with the posture of a model.

Cooling Down

During workouts, your body undergoes many changes:

- The blood flow to the muscles increases greatly.

- The blood flow to the skin and gastrointestinal tract is lessened.

- The muscles of the legs, by contracting rhythmically, help to pump blood back to the heart.

- The heart, in response to increased blood return (as well as increased metabolites in the blood and reflexes from stretch receptors) pumps faster and more vigorously at each beat.

When you stop exercising, these changes return to pre-exercise status. If you stop suddenly, some changes return rapidly and some slowly. That can bring trouble.

For example, when you stop moving, the muscles of the legs no longer help to return the blood to the heart. So don't stand around after a workout. Either warm down by walking slowly for a few minutes, or sit down on the ground with your feet out so the blood does not have to flow vertically uphill from the legs to return to the heart.

Another precaution: do not take a hot shower immediately after your workout. Heat will bring more blood to the skin, leaving less for the heart to pump to the vital organs. It might cause you to faint.

A good rule of thumb for cooling down is to do things gradually. Allow all systems to settle down evenly to the same baseline. All things physical, whether for beginnings or endings, are best done gradually.

Stretching

Let's look at an average good workout. The muscles contract to move your limbs against the resistance of body and earth many hundreds of times. That sort of rhythm and cruise can make the muscles very touchy for the rest of the day. Any slight stimulus—an unexpected bending or turning—can bring on a muscle spasm severe enough to cramp your style.

The remedy is stretching. Stretching is best done after warming down. The stretches should be repeated a couple

(continued)

Cooling Down—*continued*

of times later in the day just to remind the muscles that you won't put up with any mischief from them.

Some sports, such as gymnastics and pole vaulting, use many muscles strenuously and in several different directions. These sports need a variety of different stretches afterward. Walking is different, more unidirectional, and it gives serious resistance work to only a few major muscle groups. Moreover, these muscles are large and walking does not tax them to their limits. It is no wonder that walking is virtually injury-free. For these reasons, walking needs only a few basic stretches.

Walking, properly done, is powered mostly by the muscles of the buttocks and the back of the thighs—the gluteal and hamstring groups. Walking gives the calf muscles some resistance work to perform as well.

Several other muscle groups are used in walking, but these muscles do not move the whole body. They look after their own anatomical areas, and that involves lighter work. For example, the muscles of the shoulders move the arms; the muscles of the front of the thigh and the groin bring the leg forward for each new stride; the muscles of the neck support the head.

It is the muscles that move the whole body—the hamstrings and the calves—that will need the stretching. If you wish to stretch the other muscles as well, do so. That would be a plus.

Notes for Stretching:

The idea of stretching is to lengthen the muscle fibers and hold them at that length until they are conditioned not to go into spasm if they should be fatigued. Therefore:

- The stretch should be entered into slowly.

- The stretch should be held for 30 seconds.

- The stretch should be released slowly.

Stretch One: For the back of the thighs, the buttocks, and the lower back.

From a standing position, slowly bend forward at the waist and hang down toward your toes.

Stretch One—for the hamstrings, but-tocks, and lower back. Hold stretch for 30 seconds.

Your legs should be straight, knees unbent.

Allow only the weight of the upper body to affect the stretching rather than using strong muscular effort to try to touch your toes.

You should feel the stretching tension, especially at the back of the legs and the lower back.

Balance your weight evenly on your feet, neither too far forward on your toes nor too far backward on your heels.

Remain stretched for 30 seconds.

Slowly return to standing.

Stretch Two: For the calf muscles.

Place both hands on one knee and bring other leg back so one foot is about 24 inches behind the other.

(continued)

Cooling Down—*continued*

*Stretch Two—for the calf muscles.
Hold stretch for 30 seconds each leg.*

The heel of the back foot should be flat on the ground, and the lower part of the front leg should be vertical.

Advance the hips slightly forward until you feel that the calf muscle of the back leg is stretched.

You may press against the forward knee to help the stretching.

Remain stretched for 30 seconds.

Slowly release by bringing the hips back.

Repeat this stretch for the other calf.

Stretch Three: An optional stretch for the upper back and neck.

Grasp your right elbow with the left hand and your left elbow with the right.

Bend your head and shoulders forward with your chin on your chest.

You should feel the muscles of your neck and upper back under stretch.

Remain stretched for 30 seconds.

Release slowly.

Stretch Three—for the upper back and neck. Keep chin close to chest and hold the stretch for 30 seconds.

(continued)

Cooling Down—*continued*

Stretch Four—for the groin. Hold the stretch for 30 seconds each side.

Stretch Four: An optional stretch for the groin.

Place one knee on the ground 18 to 24 inches behind the other foot.

Using the fingers of each hand on the ground for balance, bring your head and shoulders up and your pelvis down and forward until you feel a stretching tension in the groin of the outstretched back leg.

Remain stretched for 30 seconds.

Slowly release.

Repeat for the other side.

These stretches are easy to do. You do not have to be a

contortionist or an athlete to do them. Do your stretching after each workout. It will prevent cricks and knots and cramps. Stretching also promotes flexibility, and flexibility is a good part of overall physical conditioning.

Some athletes don't bother to stretch because it's a bit of trouble and, after all, they've never been injured. Well, let me tell you about Jane Brody, a science writer for the *New York Times*. Jane had been a runner for years (how silly when she could have been a walker), and being a slim, small person she thought she was not at risk. Then, one day her feature, "Personal Health," was totally devoted to stretching and its benefits. What prompted the article was her bending down at an awkward angle to pick up something, and her back giving out in a paroxysm of pain. The article told how she had been a strong runner and began to think of herself as invulnerable until her back was seized by the gremlins of spasm. For weeks after that, she could not run.

Jane Brody became a stretching zealot. It is a good practice to follow.

When you have completed Level Two of my Walking Program, you will be at the halfway mark in your quest for fitness.

It has been an easy four weeks, all told. I am sure you have had no great trouble with the three things that count most—frequency, distance, and intensity. The regularity of three to four times a week has been simply a matter of working out the scheduling. The weekly increases in walking time have been gradual and well tolerated. The brisk pace has become increasingly easier to maintain for a full 33 minutes.

Only form, so far, may have held its frustrations for you. But improving form involves changing the patterns of walking that have become ingrained for a lifetime. Level Two has given you a basic grace, and you can go on from there to polish the rough edges.

On your way to your goal, you have already become stronger, tougher, and more confident. What fine rewards!

References

Barnard, R. James, Gerald W. Gardner, Nicholas V. Diaco, Rex N. MacAlpin, and Albert A. Kattus. "Cardiovascular Responses to Sudden Strenuous Exercise—Heart Rate, Blood Pressure, ECG." *Journal of Applied Physiology,* June 1973, pp. 833–37.

Conley, Douglas L., and Gary S. Krahenbuhl. "Running Economy and Distance Running Performance of Highly Trained Athletes." *Medicine and Science in Sports and Exercise,* vol. 12, no. 5, 1980, pp. 357–60.

Conley, Douglas L., Gary S. Krahenbuhl, Lee N. Burkett, and A. Lynn Millar. "Following Steve Scott: Physiological Changes Accompanying Training." *The Physician and Sportsmedicine,* January 1984, pp. 103–6.

Foster, C., D. S. Dymond, J. Carpenter, and D. H. Schmidt. "Effect of Warm-Up on Left Ventricular Response to Sudden Strenuous Exercise." *Medicine and Science in Sports and Exercise,* vol. 14, no. 2, 1982, p. 157.

Hagberg, James M., and Edward F. Doyle. "Physiological Determinants of Endurance Performance as Studied in Competitive Racewalkers." *Medicine and Science in Sports and Exercise,* vol. 15, no. 4, 1983, pp. 287–89.

Shellock, Frank G. "Physiological Benefits of Warm-Up." *The Physician and Sportsmedicine,* October 1983, pp. 134–39.

Chapter 3

Shady Lanes and Measured Miles

Stepping Out to Level Three

Level Three calls for a modest increase in your walking time and encourages a brisk pace. Each workout of Level Three will be 45 minutes.

Walking at a good pace for 45 minutes will take you close to the 3-mile mark, perhaps a little over. Three miles! And on your own two feet! Would you ever have thought it possible when you first started my Walking Program?

Three miles is a respectable distance in anyone's book. You will probably need to plan a route that is more interesting than circling the same block nine or ten times. You certainly should have a longer loop once in a while. You might even like to have a different course for each workout of the week just for variety.

Wherever you live—in the city, on a farm, or somewhere in between—you have numerous choices. The obvious ones such as park trails and little-used country roads are only a small part of the great variety of walks that are open to you. Look around with an imaginative eye and you will find pathways that were not meant primarily for walking. How about bridges, beaches, and golf courses for starters?

On the Town

In the cities, parks are a natural setting for walking. Our nation's capital city has parks everywhere. The path beside the Tidal Basin and the trails along the gorge in Rock Creek Park are but two of many walking paths. Washington is like a city within a park.

Pittsburgh has dozens of parks for walking, and their trails vary in length from less than a mile to over 6 miles. Detroit has over 5,000 acres of parkland, including a large island park right in the middle of the Detroit river.

All across the land, every city contains parks for walking. Atlanta has, in addition to Peachtree Street, Adams Park with its fine cross-country trail. In Chicago, the rim of Lake Michigan provides a magnificent shoreline walk, and Chicagoans also enjoy a string of parks from Gompers Park in the north down to Calumet Park in the south. Cleveland has an emerald necklace of parks around the city.

In the West, Tacoma's Point Defiance Park includes walking trails with views of Puget Sound and the Olympic Mountains. San Francisco is known not only for Telegraph Hill, but also for Golden Gate Park.

In the East, New Yorkers find parks in each of the five boroughs. Van Cortland Park in the Bronx has a well-known cross-country trail. Forest Park in Queens has many walks, including its semisecret Nature Trail. Staten Island's Clove Lake Park includes a pleasant path around the lake. Manhattan's Central Park is an 840-acre oasis in a land where glass and steel cliffs shade the numbered valleys below. The park's 6-mile drive is closed to auto traffic on weekends, and then, hundreds of people flock there on bicycles and skates and in running and walking shoes to claim the park. On a good day they may number in the thousands. Central Park is home to two walking clubs—The New York Walkers Club and The Metropolitan Racewalkers. Many independent walkers work out on their own.

In my bailiwick of Brooklyn, I am partial to Prospect Park. Like Central Park, it is closed to traffic from Friday evening to Monday morning, but unlike Manhattan, the leg power people of Brooklyn come out to the park in rather modest numbers. They come from many neighborhoods in the borough, both near and far removed. Yet, they all consider it their own neighborhood park. One fellow actually considered the park his home. One springtime Sunday, I decided to vary my workout course to include one of the cross roads. As I came to the high point of Hill Drive, I looked to the left and saw a man sitting on a beach chair, reading a book. I thought it was an unusual place to enjoy a day in the park, as Hill Road is not near any entrance or special point of interest. He must have liked the solitude. I saw him again the following week—same place, same beach chair. The next time I did a workout in Prospect Park you may be sure I included Hill Road in my planned route. Yes, he was there. To his side, a shirt was draped over some shrubbery, airing out. Slightly down the hill behind him was a 4 ×

8 piece of plywood that served as a lean-to. Why, the man was actually living in the park! He didn't look like one of New York's homeless. Rather, he was young, about 30 years old, wore metal rim glasses, and looked intellectual. He could have been a social worker or a school teacher. He lived in the park well into October of that year, and I think it was out of choice.

And why not? He was a citizen and it was his park. We others who also claim the park as our own have courage only to travel its pathways. For me, the pathways are enough for now. The 3⅓-mile loop and the cross roads provide an abundance of variety and interest.

At the southern end, there is a good-sized lake that is home to scores of waterfowl. On the east side there is a small patch of land that is used as a makeshift soccer field by a group of West Indians. Every Saturday and Sunday they set up a pair of trash cans as goals at each end of their turf and choose up sides for some hard-fought games. A little farther north the roadway passes the Prospect Park Zoo and winds its way up Battle Pass Hill, where General George Washington and his troops engaged the redcoats at the start of the Battle of Long Island. To the east of Battle Pass Hill is the gardenlike Vale of Cashmere where migrating birds often stop to rest their wings. To the west is the Long Meadow, a wide, grass carpeted valley that marks the farthest advance of the glaciers of the last Ice Age. The Long Meadow is a favorite place for family outings, kite flying, and Frisbee playing—all visible while walking along the roadway.

There is not only a diversity of activity and topography, there is also a great variety of plant life. The park is practically an arboretum, graced by tulip trees, weeping beeches, a female ginkgo, sweet and sour gum trees, hornbeams, and a 100-plus-year-old Camperdown elm.

All across the nation, each city has its parks, and each park has its own special features. Brooklyn has no monopoly on character. Your hometown surely has a park that can be special for you.

The cities have many places other than parks for walking. Look in on the quiet neighborhoods where traffic is sparse. There are out-of-the-way, residential neighborhoods that are ideal for weekday and evening walking.

Even New York City, a metropolis devoted to rush hours and double parking, keeps several neighborhoods hidden away from the internal combustion engine. My friend Roy lives in Queens and tells me that his neighborhood is so peaceful that when he does a long training run on the nearby streets, he sets out five cups of water on the trunk lid of his car and drinks a cupful on every 2-mile circuit. The cups are never disturbed by passersby. Roy is pretty clever about preventing dehydration in a quiet neighborhood. Someday he will also be wise enough to switch from running to walking.

In Brooklyn, Mimi and Sam are walkers. They have found that the east-west streets of the Manhattan Beach neighborhood near Sheepshead Bay are ideal for their workouts. Manhattan Beach is a peninsula only three blocks wide. It is about a mile and a half from West End Avenue to Kingsborough Community College and back, and traffic is so rare they get an uninterrupted workout. Brooklyn has half a dozen other neighborhoods that are equally peaceful. And Brooklyn is only one of five boroughs. If New York has its quiet places, other cities must have them too.

Exercise walking in a residential area yields another benefit. It establishes a presence on the streets and reclaims a sense of neighborhood. Where people are visible, crime declines. Where people are walking, traffic slows down, and drivers find other streets where they can travel with more abandon.

Waterways

When you are streetwise and know the park haunts and would like some place new and different, most cities are ready to accommodate you with pathways for a change of pace.

Many cities border on a body of water. The first settlers looked for a coastline site with a good natural harbor. If inland, they sought a free flowing river where there would be power to run mills. Canals were built between cities. The shores and banks of these bodies of water are now within city limits, but they are spiritually far away from the cities' rush and seething.

In our nation's capital, a good water walk is the Chesapeake and Ohio Canal, starting right in town and leading northwest far into Maryland. The original towpath is still there, but now it serves two-legged creatures. Another water walk is in the middle of the Potomac River. There, Theodore Roosevelt Island offers over 3 miles of walking trails.

Philadelphia is nestled between two rivers. The walkways along the Schuylkill River are extraordinary for their scenery. Elsewhere in Pennsylvania there are canals, dating from pre-railroad days, that link many cities in the state. There are over 1,000 miles of canals in all, and many of the original towpaths are still there for the walking.

New Jersey, in its early days, built the Delaware and Raritan Canal connecting the two rivers and giving Trenton access to New York harbor. Much of the distance along the canal is still good for walking.

New York, for all its image of concrete and cold steel, is softened by the waters of its rivers and bays. Two of the five boroughs (Manhattan and Staten Island) are islands, and two others (Brooklyn and Queens) are part of a larger island. There are untold miles of waterfront.

You can walk beside the water, or you can walk right over the water on some of the bridges. On weekends, the famous Brooklyn Bridge serves both sight-seeing walkers and exercise walkers. On weekdays, there are many commuters who prefer feet to wheels during rush hour. A little further north in uptown Manhattan, the George Washington Bridge crosses high over the Hudson River, giving walkers a wondrous view of the great river and the Palisades.

If the bridges seem too tame, you can take an alpine cable car from Manhattan's East Side to Roosevelt Island in the East River. The seldom-used roadway around the island has the most spectacular views of the New York skyline. They are as awesome today as they were 28 years ago when I spent my internship year at the island's City Hospital.

Beaches for barefoot walking are available in Staten Island, the Bronx, Brooklyn, and Queens. There are boardwalks if you don't like sand between your toes.

The middle of Manhattan has a waterside path—1½ miles around the reservoir in Central Park.

In truly upstate New York, the old Erie Canal (dourly named the New York State Barge Canal) still operates between Troy and Buffalo. The canal passes through the cities of Schenectady, Utica, and Rochester on its way across the state, and there are many places where the banks of the canal make for good walking.

In Massachusetts, the Charles River has short riverbank walks in downtown Boston and longer scenic ones on the Cambridge side toward Harvard University.

The water walk story is the same in other cities on the Great Lakes, the Gulf of Mexico, the Pacific Ocean, and the great rivers. There are water walks in Baltimore, Chicago, Dallas, New Orleans,

St. Louis, San Francisco, Seattle . . . in cities from Minneapolis to San Antonio and Provincetown to Pebble Beach.

There is magic in a flowing river that has both the vigor of youth and the longevity of centuries, a river that constantly passes by, yet still remains.

There is magic in ocean waves that rush shoreward at speeds of 15 knots simply by rising and falling. There are the mood changes of lakes from dawn till dusk. Somewhere in your city there is a waterside walk. Try to include it in your weekly schedule. The walking will change the ways of your body, and the waterforms will bring a sense of wonder to your spirit.

Out of Town

Walking places in the suburbs are much like those of the urban areas with a few additions. The suburbs, like the cities, have parks both large and small. They also have little-used back roads. Some suburbs have beaches, some have river trails.

A special feature of some suburbs is the drainage basin. There is usually a grassy strip or a sidewalk around the perimeter that can serve well for walking.

Another territorial imperative in the suburbs is the shopping mall. I personally do not like to walk where there are more people than there is total personal space. Yet, I know that a mall may be the only place to walk when the skies have opened in deluge and the Keeper of the floodgates has forgotten to close them for a few days. A mall is a good place during very hot and very cold weather. It is also a safe place after dark. Of course, walking into the mall and stopping to browse in a bookstore doesn't count as exercise time.

I know a woman of middle years who walks in a mall because she feels safe there. She walks for reasons of slimness. At first she had difficulty in passing by the food shops. There they were, all beckoning—cheeseburgers, pizza, cold drinks, and especially hot fudge sundaes. Then she devised a magic mantra to ward off all spirits of the appetite. As she would walk by each shop she would repeat to herself, "Poison, poison, poison."

The suburban planners have also designed another order of places that are good for walking, but are not made of plastic and neon. They are the nature centers, aboretums, preserves, conservancies, botanical gardens, and other variations on the theme.

Each is likely to have abundant acreage and many paths. Many have unusual specimens of plant life to please the eye. Take care that they don't distract your attention from walking form. Save your sight-seeing for the cooling down phase.

The Boondocks and Tooleydinks

The searching out of walking trails in the cities and suburbs gives you little awareness of what exists out there beyond the population centers. The farmlands and woods, the mountains and plains that make up rural America are widely disparate. There are desert trails in the Southwest. There are barrier islands to walk in the East. In some places great differences in topography are close together.

In Maine's North Woods, Baxter State Park offers spectacular trails on Mount Katahdin. Not far away on the coast of Maine, Acadia National Park has trails that overlook Penobscot Bay and its panorama of islands.

Washington State's Olympic National Park is another area of contrasts. Within a few miles there are beaches, rain forests, and mountain ridges—all with grand trails for walking.

Shore Walks: Breezin'

There is an old Massachusetts law that allows a man to walk across any beach, public or private, if he is carrying a fishing rod. The law dates back to a time when the sea provided much of the sustenance for New England families.

Beaches still invite fishing. Surf casting is sport for the hardy, and the prizes are large—striped bass from the Atlantic and salmon from the Pacific. But beaches are also for picnicking, bird watching, and walking. As long as you walk on the shore below the line of flood tide you should not be challenged. Custom and statute generally hold that the land below highest tide is no man's land and, thus, every man's land. Most states bordering on the eastern and western seas recognize this universal claim and allow you to walk on tidal beaches without violating trespass laws. Besides, it's easier to walk on firm tidal sand than on the soft private sand higher up from the water.

On the East Coast, the rockbound shoreline of Maine has relented south of Portland, and there are several fine beaches curiously alternating British and Native American names—

Kennebunk, Wells, Ogunquit, and York. The beaches continue through New Hampshire and upper Massachusetts. Then there is the Cape Cod National Seashore with four marked trails and plenty of unmarked space to breeze about on your own.

Other beaches to the south are also spectacular enough for National Seashore labels: Fire Island, Sandy Hook, Assateague Island, Cape Hatteras, Cumberland Island, and Cape Canaveral. There are many other beaches that are wonderful—town beaches, state parks, and beaches belonging to private associations. All together they number in the hundreds among the 14 states on the Atlantic coast. The sand is no respector of man's political jurisdictions; and beach walks are health giving whether federal, state, or local.

Beach Notes

The travel ads may show a carefree couple on a powder sand beach, but the reality of beach walking is not to be taken so lightly. Sand is yielding and makes for heavy exercise. You can cut your walking time by a third and still have a good workout.

Be aware, as well, that the ground is not level. The slope of the shore will place additional stress on the muscles and ligaments of one side of the body. The solution is to alternate directions. You can plan out different routes to keep your body's muscles in balance. If you are fairly strong, it may be enough to walk in one direction for 50 percent of the time, turn around and return for the remaining 50 percent of the time. Another strategy is to walk one way for 25 percent of the time, turn about, walk the other direction 50 percent of the time, turn again and return to the start for the remaining 25 percent. Almost any directional change you devise will serve the purpose.

The Great Trails

Coastal beaches are like a mere pencil line when compared to the vast canvas presented by the interior lands of this nation. Within its boundaries are several mountain ranges in haut relief. There are the great river basins, forests, plains, and even a painted desert. The frontiersmen and pioneers found pathways and passages in the natural topography of the land. As these trails were more and more traveled they became well established. Several are now Historic Trails. Some of them, such as the Santa Fe Trail, predate the birth of the states they cross. Others were developed more recently.

In the East the best known of the Great Trails is the Appalachian Trail. The first section (or the last, depending on which way you are traveling) is from Mount Katahdin south to the small town of Monson, Maine. There, the Trail is in virtual wilderness, skirting mountains and crossing streams. That first 115 miles must seem interminable. I have been on outings in Maine where the trail came through and have met hikers whose eventual destination was Georgia. They always asked the same question, "How much farther to Monson? I haven't had a hot shower for days."

As it continues farther south the Trail is not as far removed from civilization. It crosses many roads and passes through an occasional town; and so it is available to many people who live in nearby rural areas.

The Appalachian Trail may not be the best choice for routine exercise walking, but an occasional longer hike at a slower pace will give your Walking Program a nice touch of variety.

In the West, the Pacific Crest Trail wends its narrow way more than 2,000 miles from Mexico to Canada. The landscape of the Pacific states is much more rugged than that of the Appalachian Trail country, and the hiking is rather challenging. Yet, there are parts of the Crest Trail that require no rock scrambling and no bushwacking. Some of these less demanding sections are accessible at a number of points along the length of the Trail.

Other long trails run hundreds and hundreds of miles, paying little mind to state boundaries. The Lewis and Clark Trail begins at St. Louis and doesn't stop until it reaches the Pacific coast. The Santa Fe Trail connects Iowa and New Mexico. The Natchez Trail runs from Tennessee through Mississippi; the Oregon Trail, from Missouri to Oregon; and the Long Trail, through the length of Vermont between Massachusetts and Canada.

Some of the Great Trails have hiking clubs as godparents. The Appalachian Mountain Club, for example, not only plans hikes and field trips but also maintains trails. The Trails Committee takes this responsibility so seriously that some members individually take on the maintenance of a small section.

In Vermont, the Green Mountain Club looks after the Long Trail with uncommon dedication.

On the West Coast the Pacific Trail Conference coordinates the efforts of the clubs that care for the Pacific Crest Trail.

The Noncelebrity Trails

The Great Trails get the publicity, but they are only a small part of the trails available to walkers across the nation. Indeed, some of the less-than-great trails have also been adopted by hiking clubs and naturalist organizations.

The New York and New Jersey Trail Conference cares for a network of trails that cross and lead into the Appalachian Trail.

The Mountaineers Club in Washington State is the guardian for dozens of trails on and around Mount Rainier.

The Audubon Society, the Sierra Club, and the Nature Conservancy each provide care for several natural areas and their trails.

The United States Forest Service and the National Park Service, the last two of the small-time spenders among government agencies, keep thousands of miles of trails in good shape.

The Hearts Content Trails in the Allegheny National Forest, the gentle trails of Shenandoah National Park, the fantastic trails in the Badlands of North and South Dakota, the trails of the Grand Canyon, Yellowstone, the Tetons, Bryce Canyon, Yosemite Valley, and over 400 more are under the guardianship of the federal government. All the trails are superb for supplement walks in your exercise program. If you are fortunate enough to live near any of the National Park or Forest trails, they can be used on a more regular basis. As a bonus, you will be receiving a return for your tax dollars.

State and county parks are even more plentiful. They are smaller than the national parks and forests for the most part, but they are generally well cared for and often include some interesting natural features. Two state parks are worth special mention.

New York's Adirondack State Park/Forest, 2 million acres in size, is grand and spectacular, and no doubt would have been drafted as a National Park if New York State hadn't been there first. The Adirondacks have trails of every description and every level of difficulty, each with its own individuality. Hikers have long felt an attachment to the region, often having personal favorites among the trails. For these enthusiasts it was not enough to leave the well being of "their" trails entirely in the hands of a state agency. Some years ago they banded together to form the

Adirondack Mountain Club and have since looked after the trails as they might look after their children.

The second state park that is special is the Palisades Interstate Park. It is a narrow strip of land along the west bank of the Hudson River, insignificant in total acreage but including the magnificent Palisades Cliffs. There are two trails, each extending 13 miles north from the George Washington Bridge. One trail is along the riverbank at the foot of the towering rock walls of the Palisades. The other trail is in the heady atmosphere high above the river from which you can visually gather a large reach of the Hudson Valley.

The government trails are wonderful for walking—a boon for fitness and often a delight for the senses. But do not overlook the private sector. The timber companies held large parcels of forest land and built networks of woods roads for tree-cutting operations. The companies usually keep their roads in good repair even when not in active use. It is a tacit invitation to walkers. These roads may not see a vehicle for days, but you may have to share the solitude with other species of pedestrians—rabbits, deer, and moose. You won't have any quarrel with deer or smaller animals. But a moose at 1,000 pounds or more traditionally has the right of way over a walker. Most moose will neither drive you off the road nor bolt for the woods themselves. It is a rare experience to stand 100 feet from this majestic beast, each of you taking the measure of the other. After a short time the moose will amble off as if to say, "I'm leaving now—I have more interesting things to do than just stand around watching a poor creature with only two legs." Then you can resume your workout and hope you are not a bother to any other natives.

There is another type of real estate where you can find trails that are ideal for walking. They were designed as true trails, but only for wintertime use. Yes—the cross-country ski trails. In summer and autumn they are fine for exercise walking and are easier to negotiate without those long boards strapped to your feet. Some cross-country ski areas are in state and county parks. These are almost universally open for hiking after the snow melts and the ground firms. Other cross-country ski areas are in private hands. They are usually well maintained and offer a good variety of loops and distances in the warmer months as well as in the winter.

If you have a bit of explorer's blood in your veins, you can search out your own trails. The federal government will even assist you with geological survey maps that show not only hills, dales, lakes, and marshes, but also abandoned roads and substantial cowpaths. These enlargement maps have a scale of miles and contour lines so you can have a good idea of whether you will be walking on hilly terrain or flat land. You can even figure out whether a nearby stream is lazy and meandering or rushing impatiently in rapids and waterfalls. Geological survey maps are usually available in small towns at general stores. In large cities, you will have to visit a specialty bookstore. If all else fails, write to the Geological Survey in Washington, D.C.

All told, the number and variety of walking trails from coast to coast is so large it would take many lifetimes to travel them all. Walking News Inc. (P.O. Box 352, Canal St. Station, New York, NY 10013), which publishes and distributes maps, guides, and outdoor books, has several pages of lists of trail books. Some of the books describe many trails — *One Hundred Hikes in the North Cascades* and *One Hundred Favorite Trails: Great Smokies and Blue Ridge.* There are the *Fifty Hikes* books of each of the New England states, save Rhode Island, and *Fifty More Hikes* books.

Whether you live in a city, in a suburb, or in a rural area, there are trails all around. Find a favorite walk or several favorites. There are enough paths to choose a different one for every walking day of the week and special ones for weekends and holidays.

In the Old Country

Vacations are all the more reason to keep up your regular walking schedule. Walks abroad can be as fascinating as in the United States. Not only is there trekking in Tibet, but there are fjord walks in Norway, Black Forest walks in Germany, canal walks in Holland, and Champagne walks in France.

I remember a vacation in the mountain region of France and Switzerland that I enjoyed some years ago. On one leg of the trip the bus traveled along the road just to the east of Lake Annecy. I looked out the window and gasped at the vision before my eyes. In the foreground were vineyards, neatly planted as if for beauty as much as for the wine grapes. My eyes leaped to the blue waters of the lake and to awesome Mount Blanc in the near background. I knew at that moment that I must return someday and walk every trail at Lake Annecy.

Great Britain is another land of walks and walkers. The British jealously safeguard public access to trails and byways, even those that cross private estates and farms. The watchdogs of the

"Commons, Open Spaces and Footpaths Preservation Society" know their precedents in English Common Law and fiercely defend every Englishman's right to walk the land. In return the walkers accept the responsibilities that accompany these rights. They show respect for the land and for the landowners from whom they have extracted rights of way. They urge fellow walkers to "fasten all gates," to "keep to public paths across farmland," to "use gates and stiles to cross fences and walks," and to "make no unnecessary noise."

Many Europeans are superbly conditioned walkers and can do a "ramble" of many miles. When you have completed my Walking Program and continue to make walking a part of your lifestyle, you will be able to do a brisk 5 miles or 10 kilometers (6.2 miles) with members of the Swiss Alpine Club or *Le Comite National de Sentiers de Grand Randonnee* (the French Long Distance Walkers Association). But do not try to keep up with them for 15 or 20 miles. That kind of distance requires performance training, and that is different than fitness for health.

Know Your Limits

My own experience in a walkathon is illustrative. The cause was a worthy one, and in a rash moment of trying to shame others into walking for the cause of peace, I said I would attempt 50 miles. Until that time I had never done more than 10 miles and, in fact, my usual workout was about 4 miles, but I had two months to prepare. I started with a slightly longer workout the next day and each week I increased my workout distance. The week before the event, I was doing 14 or 15 miles at a pace of just under 12 minutes per mile, and no strain. On the day of the walkathon, I started out at 6:00 A.M., and in the morning's cool, I moved along easily at 12 minutes per mile. I had a good support network from the community. There was water and orange juice every 3 miles and encouragement all along. Everything was going so easily that at 20 miles I toyed with an estimate of when I would complete the 50 miles.

Suddenly, at 27 miles, strange things began to happen. It became difficult to walk a straight line, and I could not focus my eyes well. Not the martyr type, I decided right there that it was time for rest and more fluids. Perhaps it was akin to the "wall" that marathon runners hit at 20 miles.

(continued on page 40)

The Walking Program

Level Three

Week One:
Walk for 45 minutes every other day.

Week Two:
Walk *briskly* for 45 minutes every other day.

Notes for Level Three:

- Warm up as before.

- Work on form, both by parts and by wholes. Remember, the idea is to be fluid, to be economical in the energy you expend.

- For the first week at 45 minutes, walk at the same pace as Level Two. For the second week at 45 minutes, walk a little faster, but only a little. Ideally, you should walk at a pace that you can sustain for the full distance. If you find that your pace is too fast, do not just stop in your tracks. Rather, slow down gradually, until you can think calmly about briskness instead of breathlessness.

    If the muscles at the front of your shins become painful, slow down a little. These anterior compartment muscles are fairly small and are not used much in daily activities. It will take a number of workouts over a period of time to build up their strength. Each week there will be less and less discomfort until you are strong and fast, and the muscles will do their job without complaint.

- After your workout, cool down slowly.

- After you cool down, stretch.

- After you stretch, smile to yourself. You can be a little smug about the distance you have gone and the pace you have kept.

Time and Place—Measured Miles

Once you have found your favorite paths for routine or variety, you may wish to concentrate on time as well as place. It is not time itself you will want to know but time per given distance. In other words, rate of speed.

You may have already wondered, "How fast is brisk?" "Brisk" can be defined in terms of miles per hour or minutes per mile. In the next chapter, which deals with Level Four, you will be given a specific rate of speed in minutes per mile as one of your exercise goals.

At the end of Level Three it will be helpful to establish what your present rate of brisk walking is. That will give you a base pace against which to measure progress in the weeks to come.

To measure your rate of briskness, you will have to check your time over a fixed distance. A mile is convenient for measuring speed in minutes per mile, no odometers or calculators needed.

Measured miles for walkers are found whenever there is a high school or college track. These oval tracks are most always a quarter mile or 400 meters around. There is only a 3- or 4-yard difference between a quarter mile and 400 yards, and so you can figure that four times around equals a mile or very close to a mile.

Most schools will gladly allow you to use the track, except when there is some formal program in progress.

Runners who are also using the track generally will encourage you with "Looking good" or "Way to go." If you are hitting a good pace, you may hear "Go for it!"

The time to time yourself is at the end of the second week of Level Three. By then, 45 minutes should bring you close to 3 miles. For purposes of measuring pace, let's plan an even 3 miles or three sets of four laps around without extended pauses between.

(continued)

The Walking Program—*continued*

Notes for Measured Miles:

To measure your speed, record your time in minutes for the first four loops and average it with the times for the second and third sets of four loops. You will be deceiving yourself if you note the time for a fast mile and then lollygag the next 2 miles without timing them.

Runners always take the inside lane, especially on the curves. It is wise as well as considerate to allow them the inside lane well before they are about to pass you.

Walking around a quarter-mile track for 3 miles can be tedium to the twelfth power. Some walkers will like the unchanging, repetitive course. But if you are not steeped in that kind of discipline, a personal headphone set tuned in to some good music will be a nice diversion.

If your time for 3 miles is close to 45 minutes (50 minutes is close to 45 minutes), you are doing well at Level Three. As the fitness factors of frequency, distance, and speed work their magic through Level Four and beyond, you will feel as if you had wings on your feet.

After 20 minutes of rest and some liquid nourishment, I was able to go on. Three miles more, then a half hour's rest, and I was ready to lead the 400 other walkers on their nonstop, 10-mile trek through the neighborhood and the park. When I completed the 40 miles, the temperature stood at 91°F.

I thought, "Forty miles is a respectable distance, and the newspaper reporter who interviewed me at 30 miles was suitably impressed even at that point." And so 40 miles was the total distance. There was no need to follow in Pheidippides' final physiological footsteps.

The lesson of the walkathon is clear. Keep to your training distance. If you must walk farther—for good reason—then slow your pace and take enough rest periods.

Chapter 4

Incentive to Exercise: Shameless Bribes

Just Cruising through Level Four

Long before Isaac Newton gave it a name and formulated its laws, inertia was influencing our universe. Observers of human nature as well as observers of the heavens know that a body at rest tends to remain at rest. Exercise is a prime example. It is much easier to sit, virtually motionless, in front of a television set with a bottle of beer in hand and watching others, than to do it ourselves.

While exercise confirms one part of Newtonian Law (a body at rest . . .), it contradicts another (a body in motion . . .). Coaches and exercise leaders will tell you that a body in motion does not tend to remain in motion. Rather, the body tends to exercise less and less until it is at rest.

Jim Fixx, the late author of the best-selling *The Complete Book of Running* (New York: Random House, 1977), recognized this tendency toward the state of repose. He wrote to the editor of the journal *The Physician and Sportsmedicine* that he was vexed over the high dropout rate among new runners. In his letter to the editor he asked the medical readership for new ideas on how to keep beginning runners from returning to their sedentary ways.

It was a question that elicited only a few answers, none of them truly satisfying.

The Research Search

Almost all exercise programs, not just running, suffer from the same attrition problem. Experts in the sports medicine field vary in their estimates of the dropout rates—anywhere from 30 to 60 percent. The researchers want to know, "What makes one person stick to an exercise program and what makes another drop out?"

The following factors were examined in a number of studies: age, sex, marital status, occupation, emotional stability, previous state of physical fitness, smoking habits, travel distance to exercise site, reason for exercising, and the differences between supervised and unsupervised workouts. Everything went into the computer.

Out came inconclusive results, inconsistencies, and dissension among the research workers. However, the research people did agree on an overview. Motivation, they concluded, was difficult to analyze, and it was even harder to predict when, where, why, and if any individual would exercise. Human behavior, they decided, was the product of many complex interactions between an individual's internal makeup and the environment. We see examples every day of how attitudes, personality, and emotions cause people to act one way rather than another. We see how our actions are influenced by surrounding air, noise, people, time constraints, and the proximity to wonderful pastry shops.

Free Enterprise

Confirmation of the dropout tendency in exercise programs comes from the privately owned health clubs and spas. They are in business to make a profit as well as to provide fitness.

For X hundred dollars per year, you can be a member, use the equipment, and participate in classes anytime you wish. The clubs have good publicity and attract new members continually. They accept all comers, often many more than they can accommodate. The crystal ball of free enterprise reveals with unfailing accuracy that once the novelty wears off and enthusiasm wanes, attendance will fall.

A new fitness club opened in my neighborhood two years ago. I spoke to one of the exercise leaders who had a good eye for numbers as well as figures. She said that the facilities—pool, sauna, exercise rooms—could keep about 300 bodies busy at work/play at any given time. Their membership, however, was well over 1,000, and no maximum had ever been set for total membership. The managers knew from their experience at other centers that the average member is enthusiastic for the first three months and then becomes too busy with other activities to keep up with fitness.

Rain, Snow, Gloom of Night, and Other Rationalizations

Most people would rather pour themselves a drink and sink into an easy chair than go out for a walk. They might feel a tug at their conscience for not being as Spartan as they should be, but they can come up with rationalizations galore for not doing a workout.

Just for fun, here is a sampler of excuses that folks have used from the Badlands of the Dakotas to the Everglades of Florida, all good and sufficient reasons for avoiding fitness. See if you can't find one or two you might have used yourself.

- It's too hot outside.
- It's too cold outside.
- It's too windy.
- If only there were a nice cool breeze.
- Exercise is boring.
- Exercise hurts.
- I hate it.
- My husband/wife thinks it's crazy (silly, stupid).
- Exercise interferes with work.
- I already do a lot of walking on the job.
- Work interferes with exercise.
- Exercise might rob me of my femininity by making me look too muscular.
- I worked hard for 40 years and now it's time to relax.
- Who can think about exercise when I have to worry about my daughter who is going to have a baby?
- The park is too far away.
- There's never a parking space near the park, and sometimes I have to walk two or three blocks from the car.
- I have no time to exercise.
- I really should exercise, and as soon as the weather gets a little warmer, I'm going to start.

- As soon as I start my new diet, I'm also going to work out.

- I get tired just thinking about exercise.

The common denominator of most excuses is that you are setting up an adversary relationship with your exercise program. It becomes a game that you will win and exercise will lose. But while you are winning the indolence race, you are losing the health and fitness sweepstakes.

The way to avoid the adversary relationship is to take on exercise as a partner. A partnership with exercise will give you a positive attitude, and attitude can make all the difference between staying fit and sinking back into sloth. Kayleen Sager, who conducts fitness workshops and classes at the Wilder Senior Citizens' Center in St. Paul, Minnesota, for senior citizens aged 65 to 95, states unequivocally that attitude is a major hurdle in motivating seniors to exercise. Once they make exercise part of their lives, though, motivation stays high. Here are some comments from the members of Kayleen's program, the Active People Fitness Class:

"I feel more alert and alive!"

"Exercise must send special juices to the brain."

"Exercise gives me a lift."

"I am more limber and I walk with a purpose." No attitude problems there.

Malkin's Magic Motivators

A positive attitude is a good start in gathering incentives to continue your Walking Program. There are also many other ways and means to keep inertia (the body-at-rest kind) off your walking trail.

The following list contains everything from psychological theory to shameless bribes. It is a list for all sports, a basket of fruitful incentives to give you motivational strength for any exercise. Walking, of course, is the best of all exercises for keeping the faith over a lifetime of fitness.

1. Avoiding Injury

Congratulations! You have already selected a safe sport. Walking is moderate exercise, and if you increase distance and speed gradually over a period of several weeks, the chances of injury are almost nil. That means you do not try out for a 20-kilometer berth on the Olympic team when your workout schedule is 12 miles a week. For each workout, remember to warm up, cool down, and stretch.

Walking is also a psychologically safe sport. It is not intimidating to novices the way other sports can be. To appreciate this advantage just picture yourself as a beginner in lacrosse, ice hockey, or polo. In walking there is no threat of failure; and, except for improved fitness, there is no concern about success.

2. No Hassles, No Tassles

Congratulations again! Walking as an exercise is convenient, low cost, and requires no special equipment or facilities. Walking trails and paths are conveniently accessible everywhere. You can, if you like, start your workout right outside your front door.

Equipment is simple: a pair of comfortable, supportive walking shoes. No need for swimming pools, one-design sailboats, ten-speed bicycles, and two-man racing shells.

Neither does walking require you to round up a team (actually two teams) of like-minded players for a ball game. Walking doesn't even require an opponent. You compete only against yourself and time and distance. Is that not cosmic?

Two years ago I realized that walking really does have a cosmic side. It is worth a small digression to tell you about an event that showed me how totally free of all concerns walking can be.

I was entered as a race-walker in a road race sponsored by the Sri Chinmoy Marathon Team. Afterward, Sri Chinmoy, himself, asked me to demonstrate the race-walking technique. I jumped at the chance to show runners that there was a sensible alternative to their chosen sport. After the demonstration Sri Chinmoy asked about walking as a sport for exercise and for spiritual sustenance. There was no discussion of stride length, heel plant, or minutes per mile. Rather, we spoke about rhythms and the flow of effort. We compared visual and mental focus during walking. Never was there a word about competition or the race that was just completed.

That day brought forth for me an additional dimension to walking. I must have known it somewhere deep, but it took an athlete with a mystical point of reference to bring the best part of walking out where I could see it.

For those of you not familiar with him, Sri Chinmoy, now in his fifties, was a leading decathlete in his native India. Now living in the United States, he promotes peaceful athletic competition by sponsoring races in many nations.

3. Life and Breath

In Chapter 5, you will learn the benefits of metabolic walking, from preventing somatic disease to being more mentally alert to slowing the signs of aging.

Knowing about the health benefits of exercise is good, but not good enough. You must also believe the medical truths with all your heart.

You must believe that walking not only reduces hypertension, but that it will reduce *your* hypertension.

You must believe that walking will lessen the risk of *your* having a heart attack.

You must believe that walking will make *you* fit and lean and keep you that way.

The proof is right before your eyes. You are only six weeks into the Walking Program and you can now do 3 miles at a brisk pace. Six weeks ago you might have had to alert the nearest ambulance service to stand by before starting such a strenuous workout. In two more weeks you will be able to walk farther and faster and be less out of breath. Your body chemistry will change remarkably. You will metabolize carbohydrates and fats more efficiently and not allow blood lipid (fat) levels to become too high. You will strengthen your heart so it will work at everyday jobs with ease.

Walking is preventive medicine. Don't wait for some medical catastrophe to include you on the wrong side of the ledger in the statistics on heart disease, stroke, diabetes, or other human illness.

When you feel the slouchies coming on to entice you out of a workout, think about one of the health benefits that is important to you. Say to yourself, "You gotta believe!"

4. Dollars and Doughnuts

Economics is strong incentive to stay in shape. If your job depends on being sleek and lovely to look at, you will be more likely to exercise regularly.

I recently interviewed Samantha, a successful model who had maintained a slim figure throughout a substantial career. Her apartment in the "Silk Stocking" district of Manhattan was spacious and well appointed. Here was a young woman of taste and means.

I asked, "Your career requires you to stay in shape. What is your secret?"

She got up from her seat and said, "Come with me." I followed her into the kitchen, where she pointed to a copy of a very substantial paycheck taped to the refrigerator door. She told me that every week she makes a copy of her new paycheck for the refrigerator so it will be fresh in her mind.

Samantha said she had a weakness for good food and, of all the ploys she has tried in order to keep out of the refrigerator, economics works best. However, food was only half of her slimness story. She also had a membership in a fitness center and worked out religiously two evenings a week, doing the entire gamut from calisthenics to Nautilus to swimming. On weekends she was usually involved with some athletic pursuit, outdoors if possible. On the two weekday nights she would accept no appointments, meetings, or dates. Those nights were sacred for exercise time. It was all in a day's work.

5. In Good Company

The sports medicine people say that supervised group exercise programs have a two to three times higher rate of compliance than individualized programs. Despite an occasional contradictory report, group sessions are probably much better attended. Group workouts that are not formally supervised but simply provide good company are just as good for motivation. The Metropolitan Racewalkers Club works out in New York's Central Park two or three times a week. There is no attendance taken, no timing of walking speed, just kindred spirits enjoying a good workout together.

Very small groups can be effective as well. How small is very small? A group of two qualifies. Just find a partner, and you are an instant group.

Careful selection of a partner can make a big difference. Here is some counsel:

- Pick a partner who walks at your speed (required).
- Pick a partner of the opposite sex (optional).
- Pick a partner you like (optional).

Having a partner will give you some small sense of responsibility for someone else. On those days when you don't feel like going out you can say to yourself, "But I can't let my partner down. She/he needs the workout."

6. Solo with Continuo

Solo walkers can have company, too. A headphone set with a favorite tape makes for a good partner in your workouts (if you stay alert to what is happening around you and you avoid traffic areas while wearing it). You may have to experiment with music of different tempos to find what is most suitable for your workout speed. See if some lively music doesn't put some pep in your step.

Another possibility is a reading from *Books on Tape.* To complete a book, you will have to listen to several 45-minute tapes.

It is good incentive for a month of workouts.

7. Spouse Support

You may be independent and have your own interests, but if your spouse is negative or just indifferent about your pursuit of fitness and health, it will be a discouragement in small ways.

In the Ontario Exercise Heart Collaborative Study, George M. Andrew and his colleagues sent out extensive questionnaires to 728 patients a few months after they had enrolled in the exercise programs that were part of the study. There were 639 responses. When the results were in, the investigators found that the dropout rate among those whose spouses were not supportive was three times as high as among those with encouraging spouses.

A cooperative helpmate can make sure that your exercise time is kept free by fending off phone calls and by looking after small chores that might take you out of the mood for exercise.

One of the best ways to enlist the support of your spouse is to entice him/her into a walking program. What could be better than togetherness?

8. Dressing the Part

Walking requires minimal equipment. All you really need is a pair of good walking shoes. But why not add a bit of verve to your chosen sport? A brightly colored warm-up suit with stripes down the sides will make you feel like an athlete. In not-so-cold weather, you can wear pastel leotards or a striped body suit and feel like a fashion plate as well. All to get you into a proper frame of mind for exercise.

9. Make a Date with Yourself

Walking when you find some free time is like finding time to re-read the classics. Something else always comes up. Walking is even worse, because if a free hour does miraculously appear, it will probably rain or snow just because you are ready to do a workout.

The answer to the dilemma is not to wait for a free hour but to plan a schedule of workouts and enter the dates on your calendar. Actually write in your own name as an appointment. Each time will be a date with yourself. You don't break dates with a V.I.P.

Consider your exercise time sacred. Nothing short of a tidal wave advancing down your favorite walking path should keep you from your appointment with fitness. In the event of a tidal wave on Tuesday, you should try to do a good workout on Wednesday.

10. Get Ready, Get Set

Set out your walking outfit an hour before your workout. Whether you have only a pair of walking shoes or an entire ensemble of shoes, polypropylene socks, shorts, T-shirt, sweat suit, and headband, place them in a conspicuous place so they will remind you not to start some other project.

Take the telephone off the hook at least 30 minutes beforehand.

Place an "out of order" sign over the doorbell before putting on your walking shoes.

Prevent any interference with your appointed rounds.

11. Warning Signs

Hand-lettered signs are a good reminder for many things—things you should do but would rather not, and things you would just as soon do . . . but not now.

For avoiding certain seductions here are some sign suggestions:

- On your favorite easy chair, "No Parking Today."
- On your liquor cabinet, "First You Must Earn It."
- On the kitchen doorway, "Exercise Restraint."

Decide what things interfere with your workout schedule. Then, make an imaginative sign and hang it in the appropriate place at the appropriate time.

12. Keeping Records and Setting Records

Some fitness folks keep records of their workouts, noting dates, distances, and times. It is a way of monitoring progress and keeping the motivation catalyst alive.

It is worth trying, and you can select the kind of record keeping that suits you best. You can record total mileage over a period of several months. You can keep a list of personal bests for a particular distance. You can record the distance and time for every workout.

Whatever records you keep, look for long-term improvement only. Do not expect each workout to be better than the previous one. There will be good days and mediocre days, just as in all other things. Month to month, though, you will amaze yourself with new-found ability.

13. Aims and Achievements

Walking goals can be almost as tricky as soccer and hockey goals.

It is easy to say, "I am going to walk three times a week, 4 miles each time. That equals 12 miles a week. Therefore, my goal for the month will be 50 miles."

But what happens if after three weeks you have only done 28 miles? That would leave one week and 22 miles in your fitness schedule, not an easy assignment even for a well-seasoned walker.

If you are very well disciplined and your life is well-structured, you may benefit from monthly mileage goals. If not, there are other goals that may be more your style.

First, a goal for each workout is essential. The goal may be in terms of distance or time. In Level Four you will be doing 1-hour workouts. By the second week of Level Four, a 1-hour workout will cover about 4 miles. It is a substantial feat. Most walkers become a little weary by the time they have passed the halfway mark. Most walkers at that point think, "Five more minutes ought to be enough to call this a workout."

One way to keep from this temptation is to set a route that takes an hour to get back to the starting point. That way you will have to do a complete workout just to return to your home, car, or meeting place.

I can give you an example from my own experience. I am a fairly well disciplined walker, but I, too, tend to slow down midway through my workout. I often think "Where does it say a workout has to be 4 miles? Why wouldn't 3 miles be enough for today?"

Occasionally, I plan a longer workout in Brooklyn's Prospect Park and set myself a course of the roadway loop (3⅓ miles) plus the lake loop (1¾ miles). Once, I did the roadway loop first. Then, before I started the lake loop, that old "Where does it say ..." temptation became too great, and I called it a day. Had I done the lake loop first, I would have been halfway through the roadway loop when the wearies came on. At that point, it would have been just as far to continue around as to turn back. I now do the short loop first when a longer workout is on the schedule.

It is also good for motivation to have a long-term goal extending over many workouts. If miles per month are not for you, try a shorter distance such as inches around your waistline or hipline. You can realistically aim for losing an inch of circumference every six to eight weeks for as long as you have inches to spare.

14. Shameless Bribes

Set up a series of rewards for yourself. Arrange the rewards with the cooperation of your spouse if possible.

There can be a reward for diligence. Three-plus workouts a week for two weeks should be worth a small gift. For every eight weeks of continued workouts, a larger gift is called for.

There can be a reward for every 50 miles logged.

If you are watching your shape, the rewards should not be of the caloric persuasion. Try a book, game, record album, or indoor plant for one of the smaller rewards. A new sweat suit or a pair of running/walking shoes makes an appropriate larger reward. Too many sweat suits? Why not a different color for each workout of the week?

15. Races

Once you have completed the Walking Program, you may wish to try for faster speeds. Many running clubs sponsor road races that you can enter as a walker, and there are a number of races that allow only walkers.

Once you send in an entry form for a race you will be committing yourself to train for it. A modicum of competitive spirit can be used for training incentive throughout the year.

It can be strong motivation. Witness my race-walking friend, Diane. I first met her at a local road race that she had entered as a walker. She took first place in the women's race-walking division. The Trevira Twosome race was to be held a few weeks later, and after some talk about walking paces and distances Diane and I decided to enter as a pair. We trained together for a few workouts, and I was very impressed by her determination and competitive drive. Diane told me that she tries to enter at least one race a month so she will have incentive to continue her regular schedule of workouts. When she doesn't enter a race for a few months, she becomes lazy.

Oh yes, the Trevira race. Diane and I, our times combined, tied with another couple for first place. The walking division had to be decided by hundredths of a second. We were declared to be in second place by 0.04 second.

Races provide another inducement to continue your training. The winners are presented with medals or trophies. Every race has different categories of awards, and usually the winners of each ten-year-age division are awarded with precious metal (nowadays, precious-looking metal). You may be completely nonmaterialist in outlook, but if you come home with gold, silver, or bronze, the high will last at least the rest of the day.

16. Teaching/Learning

When you become a strong walker and can demonstrate good form, have a try at teaching others. First of all, you will be helping them toward fitness and health. Second, you will strengthen your own motivation. When you teach, you will identify with walking and include it as part of your lifestyle.

You will also become more aware of your own form when you teach, and you will try to polish up the nuances that make for grace.

Teaching is teaching. And teaching is learning.

17. Timing

In auto racing, sailing, and selected other sports, position is everything. In walking, timing can be the key factor.

Your circadian rhythms may make you an early bird or, conversely, a night owl. Few are both. You will find there is a time of day when you feel really "up" for walking. Then, you hardly have to think of moving your legs, for they move you.

My friend Dave, who started me walking, likes to walk in the earliest hours of the morning. I prefer about 10:00 A.M. if it must be the morning at all. When he and I used to meet at Marine Park for our weekly walk together, we had to compromise on the time, and so each of us gave in 2 hours to meet at 8:00 A.M. It was well worth the time dislocation to have company and to have someone with a sharp eye to watch for form.

I find my worst time of day is around 6:00 P.M. My metabolism is at its ebb, and it is a real mental effort to put on walking shoes to start a workout. There was a time in my life, however, when I chose 5:30 to 6:30 P.M. for exercise. When I was in professional school, classes were over at 5:00 P.M., and rather than fight the hordes at rush hour, my classmate Jules and I took our bodies and swimsuits to a nearby municipal pool. The water temperature, always on the arctic side, never failed to shake out the early evening doldrums. After a good swim, there was always a seat on the train home.

If you are a 9 to 5 worker in the city, perhaps the prospect of missing rush hour can induce you to schedule an hour for walking right after quitting time. I can even give you a couple of physiologic tricks so you can by-pass the 5 o'clock blahs (see below).

18. Warm-ups for Your Mood

When your mood leans toward easy chairs and daydreams instead of swinging arms and legs, tell yourself, "Do a warm-up at least, and then decide whether or not to do a workout."

A warm-up will liven your circulation. There will be greater blood flow to the muscles and the brain.

A second method for swinging your mood in the right direction is having a cup of strong tea. Tea will give you more gumption for doing a workout. It will also lessen your perception of effort, and it will encourage your body to use a higher percentage of fat as fuel for walking. Tea is the secret of elite marathoners, but you can use it for 4-mile workouts when you'd rather be taking a nap.

Large Walkers and Walkers at Large

If you are using walking to find your true slim self within your present body, there are a couple of psychological stimuli that may help.

1. Photographs

    Tape a picture of a grossly large person to the refrigerator and add the caption, "This person didn't exercise."

    Tape a picture of a lean, strong person to the cupboard with the caption, "This beautiful person exercises every other day."

2. Reflections

    As a further stimulus to exercise, look at yourself in a full-length mirror. You must be down to bare skin, of couse, but that is not enough. It is still too easy to recognize yourself, and recognition precludes being objective. Take a paper bag large enough to go over your head and cut two eyeholes. When you look at yourself wearing only a paper bag you will see another person's body. Then you can be objective and say, "That person in the mirror really needs to exercise." Walking at a frequency of three or four times a week will help you toward stamina and slimness. In a few months, you will no longer be a large walker; you will be a walker at large.

There you have it: comprehensive lists of secrets, tricks, and commonsense initiatives to help make exercise an integral part of your lifestyle.

Use them in combinations and permutations. Write down reminders and schedules. Take all the help you can find, be it animal, vegetable, or mineral.

It is easy to fall into slothful ways; and, conversely, it is difficult to keep up with an exercise program.

Try everything. Adopt anything that helps, however silly it may sound. What works for you, pursue.

In this situation the end justifies the means. It's like promising a lad that eating his spinach will make him big and strong. It really might—and even if it doesn't, it can't hurt. Convince yourself that you must walk *this* day because today is the essential one if you are to have a better figure, a cheerier outlook, a cold-free season, the right to a rich dessert, or an expensive sweater. Maybe none of these happy rewards will materialize, but maybe they all will!

The Walking Program

Level Four

Week One:
   Walk briskly for 1 hour, three or four times a week.

Week Two:
   Walk *very* briskly for 1 hour, three or four times a week.

Notes for Level Four:

- The notes for all the previous levels apply.

- By the end of Week Two you should be walking at 15 minutes per mile or better. To check your speed, you can set a measured course of 4 miles and time yourself. You may, instead, use other measures of intensity of effort and just walk for an hour's time.

   One test of adequate effort that has been much publicized is the pulse test. Your heart rate should theoretically be 70 percent of maximum, and maximum itself is an age-graded theoretical figure. There are several other problems with the pulse test, especially in the cold weather when you wear gloves, long sleeves, and turtleneck shirts. There are easier tests.

References

Andrew, George M., Neil B. Oldridge, John O. Parker, David A. Cunningham, Peter A. Rechnitzer, Norman L. Jones, Carol Buck, Terence Kavanagh, Roy J. Shephard, and John R. Sutton. "Reasons for Dropout from Exercise Programs in Post-Coronary Patients." *Medicine and Science in Sports and Exercise,* vol. 13, no. 3, 1981, pp. 164–68.

Dwyer, J., L. McColgan, M. Rapp, J. Bonitatibus, and R. Clark. "Self-Paced Running and the Anaerobic Threshold." *Medicine and Science in Sports and Exercise,* vol. 14, no. 2, 1982, p. 128.

Several fall under the classification of "perception of effort" tests. They are accurate whether you are a beginner or an Olympic race-walker. First, you should feel you are pushing yourself a bit. Do not walk at a rate of speed that is too comfortable. Second, it should be difficult to hold an easy, prolonged conversation with your walking partner. Third, you should be slightly out of breath throughout your workout. That is not to say that you should be gasping for air every two steps, but you should be breathing faster and deeper than normally to catch your breath.

By the end of Level Four your body will start to change its chemistry and metabolic processes. These beneficial changes will not be limited to the time that you exercise. Your improved metabolism will continue for 24 to 48 hours beyond each workout.

You will also develop stronger walking muscles and greater stamina. Walking will seem less a chore and more a lifetime pastime.

Ivy, J. L., David L. Costill, W. J. Fink, and R. W. Lower. "Role of Caffeine and Glucose Ingestion on Metabolism during Exercise." *Medicine and Science in Sports,* vol. 10, no. 1, 1978, p. 66.

Jackson, Allen, Rod K. Dishman, Scott La Croix, Robert Patton, and Robert Weinberg. "The Heart Rate, Perceived Exertion, and Pace of the 1.5-Mile Run." *Medicine and Science in Sports and Exercise,* vol. 13, no. 4, 1981, pp. 224–28.

Noble, Bruce J. "Clinical Applications of Perceived Exertion." *Medicine and Science in Sports and Exercise,* vol. 14, no. 5, 1982, pp. 406–11.

Noble, Bruce J., Gunnar A. V. Borg, Ira Jacobs, Ruggero Ceci, and Peter Kaiser. "A Category-Ratio Perceived Exertion Scale: Relationship to Blood and Muscle Lactates and Heart Rate." *Medicine and Science in Sports and Exercise,* vol. 15, no. 6, 1983, pp. 523–28.

Robertson, Robert J. "Central Signals of Perceived Exertion during Dynamic Exercise." *Medicine and Science in Sports and Exercise,* vol. 14, no. 5, 1982, pp. 390–96.

Rogers, Cindy Christian. "Firing Up for Fitness." *The Physician and Sportsmedicine,* April 1984, pp. 134–42.

Sager, Kayleen. "Exercises to Activate Seniors." *The Physician and Sportsmedicine,* May 1984, pp. 144–51.

Shephard, Roy J. "Motivation: The Key to Fitness Compliance." *The Physician and Sportsmedicine,* July 1985, pp. 88–101.

Simon, J., J. L. Young, B. Gutin, D. K. Blood, and R. B. Case. "Perceived Exertion Relative to Anaerobic Threshold in Trained and Untrained Cyclists." *Medicine and Science in Sports and Exercise,* vol. 15, no. 2, 1983, p. 121.

Chapter 5

The Best Rewards

Sugar and Spice and Everything Nice—
The Walking Program for Keeps

"Sugar and spice and everything nice" is familiar to most of us as a phrase from a favorite nursery rhyme, but it is serious physiology when applied to fitness.

Sugar

Blood glucose is the basic fuel for most body functions. The brain runs on glucose; the heart runs on glucose; and so do most of the other organs of the body. The voluntary muscles with which we walk and talk and leap and laugh all operate on glucose, directly and indirectly.

Blood glucose is like an energy exchange center. The "Blood Glucose Exchange" receives new supplies of glucose from the liver, and in turn the "Exchange" supplies glucose wherever it is needed around the body.

The blood glucose level normally remains in a fairly narrow range—80 to 120 mg. per 100 c.c. of blood. If it falls too low (below 40 mg.), there is likelihood of shock. If it rises too high (over 800 mg.), there is danger of coma.

That range—40 mg. to 800 mg.—may seem wide, leaving plenty of leeway for occasional dieting and gourmet excesses. But the bloodstream can only hold a rather small amount of glucose at any one time—5,000 mg. suspended in 5 liters (more than 5 quarts) of blood. A generous slice of pecan pie might contain 300 calories or 75,000 mg. of glucose. That is 15 times the total amount of glucose in the entire blood stream! Conversely, a good workout can burn 300 calories. That 300 calories of exercise will use 75,000 mg. of glucose, which is also 15 times the amount of glucose in the entire bloodstream!

Obviously, there must be a backup source of energy to cover glucose needs during a workout. There must also be a place to store the excess glucose that comes in with a piece of pie so the bloodstream is not overloaded. This storage ability is vital to good health.

Your body has several mechanisms for handling situations in which there is too much or too little glucose. It can store glucose in the form of glycogen in both the liver and the muscles. Conversely, the glycogen stored in the liver can be changed back into glucose virtually at any time it is needed, and glycogen in the muscles can be used directly by the muscles for energy. The liver can also convert excess glucose into fat, and in times of need it can turn fat into glucose. When blood glucose rises, the insulin-secreting cells of the pancreas raise their output to help use up excessive glucose throughout the body. These are the major mechanisms that handle glucose levels; there are others.

How does walking as an exercise influence glucose balance? W. W. Wright and colleagues at Dalhousie University in Halifax, Nova Scotia, found that the systems of people who trained regularly could turn glucose into storable glycogen much faster than untrained individuals. Add to this the findings of David L. Costill, Ph.D., and researchers in Oslo, Norway, which showed that regular exercise increases muscle glycogen storage.

A. Wirth and his research team at the University of Gothenberg in Sweden found that endurance exercise improved insulin clearance by the liver. The distance athlete, thus, had a more responsive insulin-glucose system and could fine tune his/her carbohydrate metabolism.

Irene N. Sills and Frank J. Cerny at Buffalo, New York, showed that exercise improves the insulin-glucose balance when they placed a group of insulin-dependent diabetic children in an exercise program. High blood glucose levels were significantly reduced. In nondiabetic children in the same exercise program, blood glucose levels remained the same.

Other studies of carbohydrate metabolism focused on the microbiological changes with exercise, especially in the mitochondria (which are the cells' chemical factories) and the associated insulin receptors that cause the tissues to use glucose. The endurance sports caused an increase in the numbers and sensitivity of insulin receptors in many tissues of the body. Similarly, there was an increase in cellular respiratory capacity and in mitochondrial activity in muscle tissues. All the better to keep carbohydrates in their place.

And Spice

Early research in sports medicine measured aerobic power, cardiac function, and other bodily changes that occur with exercise. The investigators duly recorded their results but also noted unanticipated mental changes. Some subjects who happened to be on antidepressant medication had to reduce their dosage midway through the exercise program. Other subjects, not on medication, felt more calm and resistant to moodiness when they exercised regularly.

Then the research people talked to the athletes. The runners told about the runners' high. Swimmers told about the sense of complete relaxation after a workout.

Finally, studies were designed to check out the full range of athletic influence on mental function.

Richard A. Markoff and University of Hawaii researchers asked runners to complete a Mood Profile Questionnaire after a 1-hour run. They found a reduction in tension-anxiety, anger-hostility, and depression-dejection indices.

Arthur Weltman, Ph.D., at the University of Colorado and Bryant A. Stamford, Ph.D., at the University of Louisville found that regular exercise brought about the following psychological changes:

- a more positive mental outlook

- an improved self-image and self-concept

- a sense of accomplishment

- decreased anxiety and tension

Studies in both animals and humans have shown that there is increased tolerance to pain after exercise.

Other studies show improved performance in specific facets of learning and problem solving.

M. H. Cox and Roy J. Shephard, Ph.D., studied the effects of employee fitness programs in large institutions. They found less absenteeism, lower employee turnover, and improved attitudes toward co-workers and toward work.

Kayleen Sager, working with older people, reports that participants in her exercise programs gain self-confidence and a personal sense of competence. She notes that participants leave exercise classes relaxed and often smiling.

We find the need for exercise in psychological theory as well as in practice. And walking fits the psychological model perfectly.

Starting with the senses generally and the sense of touch and pressure (proprioception) in particular, we maintain a sense of reality through sensory stimulation. When deprived of our senses for any significant amount of time we lose all sense of time and may hallucinate.

Proprioception is the deep pressure sense of the muscles and ligaments and joints. This sense is responsible for our awareness of position, balance, and coordination. Leg contact with the ground, a constant base, gives us a sense of personal stability. Just standing around is not enough. You must move so you feel each step as a proprioceptive stimulus. Just as you do not feel whether or not you are wearing a watch a few minutes after putting it on, so you do not receive much sensory stimulation from your legs when you are standing still.

Which activity is best to keep you in touch with your limbs? Walking, of course. Running provides only intermittent contact with the ground. So does rope skipping, basketball, and hopscotch. Cycling offers no personal contact at all with the ground. Swimming takes place in a weightless environment. Walking gives your body the most contact with the ground.

Walking has another advantage for the brain. Beyond the leg contact with the ground and the stimulation of your proprioceptive sense, walking gives you rhythm.

Rhythm is a psychological need that few professionals recognize. Yet, rhythm is fundamental to all life. Your body is like the several rhythm instruments of a live band being played all at once by one musician. There are the rhythms of your daily sleep-wake cycle and the rhythms of the heartbeat, respiration, and sexual pleasures.

We all respond to the rhythms of music. The rhythms of dance capture us in movement. As you become more adept at walking you will feel a rhythm in your steps that will help you to keep a steady pace through each workout.

Walking can bring psychological strength to face other problems. My wife, Jill Reintjes Malkin, R.N., a nutritional consultant, found that exercise walking provided a breakthrough for many of her patients. Jill works with patients who have difficulty in following the diet prescribed by their physician. Patients often tell her, "I feel out of control" or "I have no will power."

The exercise walking Jill includes in their overall treatment program helps the patients to begin taking charge of their own lives. After they walk for the first time as part of the program—usually a half mile at a slow pace—they feel the beginning of a self-confidence that carries over to food preparation and mealtime habits. One small success begets another and suddenly the sun is shining.

Runner/cardiologist/philosopher George Sheehan, M.D., adds his own special views on the interrelationship of the mental and the physical. He sees running (and walking, also) as a means of narrowing the distance between "what we are and what we can be." For him, running brings the union of "reality and aspiration." He notes that self-esteem is highest when there is little difference between your actual self and your ideal.

Walking to the office with a lively stride provides excellent exercise and is a superb way to start the day.

Research and personal philosophy have their place, but the final brief for the notion that exercise leads to positive mental changes is found in the results. Let's compare the exercise enthusiast with the inactive person.

You know how nonathletes hate to walk, even to the neighborhood newsstand. When they are out for an evening, they will go to great lengths to park half a block closer to their destination.

A trained walker, on the other hand, finds the walking of everyday activities to be effortless. It is neither a mental nor a physical effort to walk an extra block or two for an errand or an appointment. Even if it is a half mile, the walker's attitude is positive: "Oh, a half mile will take me less than 10 minutes."

And Everything Nice

The rewards of walking have only begun. There are gifts of better shape, more active fat metabolism, reversal of osteoporosis, reduction of high blood pressure, lessened risk of heart attack, prevention of age decline, and keeping your appetite in check without half trying.

After these, there are a couple of surprises still to come.

The Lean Machine

Slimness is heavy on health and light on the eyes. No argument. *Becoming* slim, however, brings out a few disagreements. There are, it seems, as many methods as there are experts.

Getting down to basics, the common denominator is a balance of body fuel—the amount taken in versus the amount used up. Human fuel, of course, is in the form of food and drink. That fuel is either burned metabolically or by activity, and any that is not used is stored in the body.

To become slimmer, you can choose to eat less or burn more fuel (see accompanying table). Simple.

Which is better? Neither! It is best to do both at the same time. Here is why.

When you lose weight you can lose it in fluid, fat, and/or lean tissue (muscle, bone, etc.). Dieting and exercising produce weight loss in different ways.

- Dieting can result in substantial weight loss through fluid loss, fat loss, *and* lean tissue loss.

- Exercising brings more modest weight loss unless the exercise is long and arduous. With moderate metabolic exercise there is only fat loss. There is also slight lean tissue gain.

- Combined diet and exercise causes greater weight loss than from dieting or exercise alone. There is substantial fat loss and slight lean tissue gain.

Burning Calories

A 150-pound individual

walking at	3 mph	4 mph	5 mph
equal to	20 minutes/mile	15 minutes/mile	12 minutes/mile
burns	275 calories/hour	365 calories/hour	585 calories/hour

After each workout your body reaches a higher level of metabolism, approaching that of a naturally slim person. The effect of exercise, in terms of calorie consumption, lasts 24 to 48 hours beyond the actual exercise period.

At Stanford University Medical School, Steven Lewis and his co-workers examined a group of overweight women who had just enrolled in an exercise and weight loss program. The exercise classes were minimal—19 minutes of walk-jogging two days a week plus 1 hour of stretching and calisthenics two other days a week. (This amount of exercise seems to be at less than the aerobic threshold of frequency, time, and pace.) In addition to exercise, there was one class a week of counseling on diet control, though no specific menu was given.

After 17 weeks the women showed highly significant reduction in total body weight, somewhat *higher reductions* in fat weight, and slight increases in lean weight.

If these women could do so well with a mild exercise program with reasonable attention to diet, just think what you could accomplish with a truly metabolic walking program.

Men are luckier when it comes to exercise and slimness. They can lose weight with only minimal attention to diet if they keep exercise walking as a way of life.

Children are the most charmed of all. A good exercise program can change their basic metabolic processes so well that they will lose weight and maintain slimness even if they stop exercising for a time. The metabolic changes seem to continue on their own momentum for several months.

The metabolic ways of the body are not entirely understood, but metabolism has a great deal to do with whether you are fat or slim. For example, I know a few obese people who swear that they eat very little, yet gain weight. They say, "I get fat just watching someone else eating."

While the quote must be taken metaphorically, it is true that a 1,200-calorie diet will cause one person to lose weight and another to gain. There is reason behind the paradox.

When you start dieting and the scale shows a loss of weight, your resting metabolism will decline. This has been confirmed by several studies, but you have your own confirmation. Isn't it easy to lose weight the first few days of a new diet and doesn't it become more difficult as you continue dieting?

The tendency to settle in at a certain weight has been made into an entire school of metabolic philosophy called "set point" theory. This theory tends to oversimplify the workings of body chemistry, but it is a useful model for explaining some of the mysteries of weight gain and loss. According to the theory, your set point is the weight you normally maintain when you're not thinking about it.

Proponents of the set point theory say that you can overcome your set point temporarily with a restrictive diet, but unless you stay on that diet forever you will gain the weight back. They certainly can point to plenty of examples.

But now there is good news. Exercise can lower your set point by changing your metabolism. The weight that you settle in at can be reduced by many pounds through regular exercise. A good walking program can help you to become a naturally thin person.

Part of the original draft of set point theory held that exercisers would have a larger appetite and, therefore, would make up the calories lost at exercise. It sounded reasonable, but under scientific scrutiny, "reasonable" did not square with fact.

Studies at New York City's St. Luke's Hospital and Columbia University and at the Clinical Research Center in Harrow, England, showed that with both mild and moderate exercise, no compensatory increase occurred in ad lib food intake among overweight subjects.

Runners and walkers could have told the researchers what to expect. These people know that after a strenuous workout, appetite is suppressed severely for an hour or more. Liquids are needed desperately, but not food. Appetite returns gradually, and over the next couple of days it is in line with the needs of a slim person. If you look at the shapes of distance athletes—runners, walkers, cross-country skiers—their set points are uniformly on the side of slimness.

There is still another dimension to the idea of slimness. It is not weight loss, nor 900-calorie diets, nor 10-mile workouts. Slimness concerns shape. If you have a figure that looks good, does it matter if you weigh 10 pounds more or less? Perhaps a tape measure is a better device than a scale for judging shape. The best of all measuring instruments is the mirror on the wall.

Further insight into the shape-weight question comes in the form of the fit of your clothes. Going down one clothing size (for women) usually requires a loss of 10 to 12 pounds via diet. That same one size will need only a loss of 7 or 8 pounds if exercise is the method.

Slimness and shapeliness, however measured, are a matter of removing the fat and showing nicely curved muscles over your bones.

If you are a woman, exercise walking will not build massive muscles. Rather, it will give your muscles a pleasant form by removing the camouflaging fat and will give you a well-defined shape.

If you are a man, walking will give your muscles—legs and buttocks especially—a look of strength. Walking will also work on your waist the bulge of the front and the flabbiness on the sides. Walking will not give you a Mr. Universe outline. That comes from pumping iron. But the shape that body building gives is only that: shape. It is not fitness, and it is not health. Walking is the universal exercise for being in shape as well as being shapely.

Have a Heart

Heart disease has been studied in every way imaginable. The lives of heart attack victims have been examined minutely, from diet to exercise to heredity to personality.

When a disease threatens the lives of as many people as heart disease does, and when investigators have a large reservoir of survivors, you can bet there will be plenty of research going on. Before checking out the principal research studies, let's go over a few high points of how the heart works in health and illness.

1. We know the heart as the muscle that pumps blood to all the organs of the body, including itself. As the blood is pumped

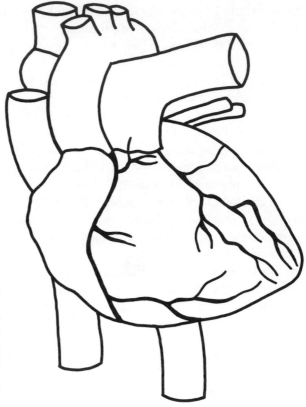

The heart and great vessels as seen from the front. The coronary arteries (in black) are the right coronary artery and the anterior descending branch of the left coronary artery. Hidden from view is the circumflex branch. The blood supply to the working muscle of the heart is delivered entirely through the coronary arteries.

through the chambers of the heart it does not supply oxygen and nutrients to the heart muscle. To get to the heart muscle the blood must enter the coronary arteries that branch off from the ascending aorta. Then the blood passes through the branches of the smaller coronary arteries and capillaries and supplies the heart muscle cells.

2. Heart muscle is not the same type of muscle tissue as regular skeletal (voluntary) muscle and has little if any capacity to work or play without oxygen. A sprinter's leg muscles can perform anaerobically for 200 yards. Then, at rest, the blood supply will bring in enough oxygen to repay the oxygen debt. The heart muscle cannot go into oxygen debt. It will refuse to pump any faster or harder than its oxygen needs permit, and it will let you know when enough is enough.

3. In coronary artery disease, lipid deposits narrow the coronary arteries and blood flow is restricted. If one of the coronary arteries, even one of the smaller branches, becomes completely blocked, a heart attack results.

4. Several factors can increase or decrease the likelihood of coronary artery constriction. The most important factors that you can control are cigarette smoking and blood lipid (fat) levels.

Many studies have shown that coronary heart disease is present much more often in people with high levels of cholesterol and triglycerides. Conversely, individuals with low blood lipid levels rarely suffer heart attacks. The studies include the Framingham study, the Brooks Air Force study, and a range of others from Hawaii to Oklahoma to Great Britain. There is virtually no dissent from anyone in medicine.

The problem is actually a little more complex than dealing with an excess of wicked old cholesterol. The cholesterol of the blood is not a solitary evil. Cholesterol exists in the blood mainly as high-density lipoprotein (HDL) cholesterol and low-density lipoprotein (LDL) cholesterol. The two are a Dr. Jekyll–Mr. Hyde pair wherein the HDL-cholesterol acts to protect the heart from the likes of the LDL-cholesterol.

Ideally, total blood cholesterol, LDL-cholesterol, and triglycerides should be kept as low as possible and HDL-cholesterol should be as high as possible.

The sports medicine people know that such an ideal blood profile is typical of athletes in endurance sports. They know, too, that exercise changes the way the body deals with fats. The logical expectation is that exercise influences blood lipid levels and perhaps affects coronary artery disease, itself.

Studies have shown this to be the case. Here is a sampling of the good news:

1. Exercise training increased coronary blood flow.

2. Moderate exercise, specifically walking, uses a greater percentage of fat as an energy source.

3. Strenuous, short-run exercise uses a greater percentage of carbohydrates as an energy source.

4. In all metabolic (truly aerobic) exercise programs, HDL-cholesterol increased.

5. In long-term, moderate exercise programs of one year or more:

   - HDL-cholesterol increased
   - LDL-cholesterol decreased
   - Total cholesterol decreased
   - Triglycerides decreased

6. With exercise training, there is a smaller rise in post-meal triglyceride levels.

7. With exercise training:

   - Blood volume increased
   - Stoke volume (blood volume pumped at each heart beat) increased
   - Resting heart rate decreased
   - Heart rate for a given work load decreased
   - Blood viscosity decreased
   - Cardiac oxygen need for a given work load decreased

8. For patients who had suffered a heart attack, a sustained program of moderate exercise reduced the incidence of a second attack by more than fourfold.

Walking for exercise is a good way to be kind to your heart. Exercise combined with a prudent diet low in animal fats, low in cholesterol, and low in simple sugars is even better for your heart.

Banking on Calcium

A teenager can climb a 10-foot fence, fall, and get up and run off as if nothing unusual had happened.

A senior citizen may trip while walking in the street and have to spend the next three weeks in the hospital for the repair of a hip fracture.

It has long been known that bone strength decreases with advancing age, especially in women after menopause. Bone strength also declines in patients who have been confined to bed rest for any reason. In recent years, space scientists have noted that astronauts have lost some mineral content of their bones during extended periods of weightlessness in space.

Bone density clearly is a use versus disuse matter as much as it is a question of age.

There is also the influence of calcium in the diet. Then there are the wild cards of vitamin D and growth hormone, both of which are needed for calcification of bone structure. Vitamin D is increased by exposure of the skin to sunlight; and growth hormone is increased by estrogen, low levels of blood glucose, *and* physical activity. Mother Nature gives very few simplistic answers.

The mineralization of bone is basic to bone strength but it is not one of the body's priorities for the use of calcium. Calcium has other, more important, *raisons d'être*. Calcium is involved in nerve impulse transmission, muscle contraction, and the blood clotting mechanism. To these ends the body maintains a fairly constant concentration of blood serum calcium and, if necessary, will draw upon the calcium from the bones of the skeleton to hold that level of blood calcium steady.

It is up to you to give those bones the raw material they need to thrive on. You must:

1. have enough calcium in your diet.

2. absorb the calcium from the gastrointestinal tract.

3. deposit the calcium into the structure of the bones.

Physical activity stimulates the bones to become highly mineralized. Several studies have shown that athletes have denser bones than nonathletes. Other studies have demonstrated that the demineralization of bone (osteoporosis) occurring in women after monopause can be reversed by exercise. In one of the studies, the findings startled the investigators. They found that running increased bone density not only in the legs, but also in the wrists and fingers! The deposition of calcium salts was not a simple matter of individual bones being stimulated by exercise. Something was happening in the biochemistry of the entire body. That something involved a number of hormones, minerals, and physiological processes. The bottom line was that exercise resulted in stronger bones throughout the body.

An incident that I remember from 22 years ago comes to mind whenever I talk about osteoporosis. I was on a horseback trip in the Rockies with the Wilderness Society. The crew included a head rider, a cook, and two trail hands, all to look after the ordinary and extraordinary details of life at 8,000 to 11,000 feet in the White River National Forest. Besides the regular crew, there was a leader emeritus who was tougher than all the rest. Eighty-year-old Pop slept out in the open in his blanket roll while the rest of us were in tents. He often rode along the side of the trail where the terrain was rough when he needed to move ahead of a few horses. He was also on his own two feet a great deal, looking after the horses and equipment and just plain checking around.

One day was a rest day at a particularly scenic campsite. After the noon meal, Pop decided to do a little riding just for the exhilaration of being out under an infinite sky on what seemed to be the top of the world. At one point he was riding across the steep banks of a narrow stream when the horse lost its footing and stumbled. Pop was pitched forward onto the ground. One of the trail hands saw him fall and rushed to his aid. In a matter of seconds, six people were at the scene, but Pop was already on his feet and going after his horse. He could not understand what all the commotion was about.

At 80 years of age, Pop had bones that were mineral strong.

How Old Is Old?

S. J. Perelman once wrote a book entitled *The Road to Miltown, or Under the Spreading Atrophy* (New York: Simon and Schuster, 1957). He did not know how appropriate the title would be to the question of aging.

In general, old people are physically weaker, slower, less steady, and less flexible, and have less stamina than others. At the same time that these changes of aging occur, people become less physically active. Does age cause decline, or does disuse bring on the signs of aging?

The answer can be found by observing a special group of people who have become chronologically older but not less active. They are the athletes in the Masters Sports programs. They compete against others of their own age, and their performances by age group are astounding. Fifty-year-olds are running the mile in 4½ minutes. Fifty-five-year-olds are pole vaulting close to 14 feet.

Microscopic examination of muscle fibers taken by biopsy from some of these Masters athletes shows relatively few structural changes when compared to the tissues of well-conditioned young people.

It is only when we compare the performance records of elite athletes in their 20s with the Masters athletes that we see an obvious decline. That decline, however, is less than half of what is seen in people who do not include physical activity in their lives.

Tension and Hypertension

Most human illnesses announce themselves. An abscess causes swelling and pain. Allergies cause stuffy noses and rashes. Middle ear infections cause dizziness. Viruses can cause nausea, diarrhea, muscle pain, and/or several other loud symptoms. But hypertension (high blood pressure) is a quiet affliction. It causes no discomfort or other symptoms in its early stages. But when hypertension decides to make itself known, it does so dramatically—with a blowout of one of the blood vessels of the brain.

Strokes occur at least twice as frequently in people with hypertension as in others. Therefore, we must not ignore hypertension just because it hasn't been a bother yet.

Much research has been devoted to finding the cause of hypertension. The idea was to isolate the cause and then produce a cure. As the results came in, it seemed as if every study uncovered a new cause: hardening of the arteries; oversecretion of various hormones associated with the kidneys and adrenal glands; life stress levels; and then hereditary predisposition. In many cases, no cause could be identified, so these cases were simply labeled "essential hypertension." And the research goes on to this day.

Fortunately, the development of treatment did not wait for the causes of the disease to be neatly pigeonholed. Early on, researchers found that a low-salt diet helped to lower high blood pressure, and salt restriction is still a cornerstone of treatment.

Weight loss in the obese was a second method of reducing blood pressure.

Then came the diuretics and the antihypertensive drugs.

Finally, the medical profession accepted exercise. Studies of both humans and animals showed that exercise at metabolic levels will bring down high blood pressure.

A British study, reported in *Lancet,* found exercise more effective than sodium restriction for controlling blood pressure levels. Of course, a combination of the two was better than either one alone.

Observations of women in a Dallas study showed that it is not weight reduction per se that brings about a reduction of blood pressure, but rather a lower ratio of fat to lean tissues. Exercise, of course, will alter that ratio much more effectively than diet.

Another study in St. Louis looked at adrenaline levels, which are implicated in hypertension. The investigators found that adrenaline levels normally increased during heavy work and exercise, but that increase was minimized in individuals who were exercise trained.

Walking is the best exercise because it is moderate in intensity and causes the least blood pressure rise during workouts. Short, intense exercise and especially isometrics and weight training can cause marked blood pressure rises during peak activity.

Special Effects

The scientists have been able to document the rewards that walking brings to the body's tissues and organs. But there are other benefits of walking that have to do with the quality of life and that are elusive to research. Yet, they are real and can play an important role in your life.

Energy

One of the special rewards of gaining fitness is an increased sense of vitality. It is a paradox that by spending energy you will gain more energy. We have seen it with Kayleen Sager's senior citizens who feel more alive and are ready to tackle projects commonly associated with the young. It is true of corporate personnel enrolled in fitness programs. Instead of taking the two-martini lunch after which nothing productive is done for the rest of the day, employees whose lives include metabolic exercise will do a solid afternoon's work, and do it in good spirits.

As you gain a good level of fitness, you will also gain the mental and physical energy to do more in a day than many who are ten years younger.

A Plague of "No Parking"

John is a good friend whose field is theoretical mathematics. He is also a good walker who works out regularly. He has a supple stride that reels in the miles at 10 minutes each. Math and walking had nothing to do with each other until one day a third interest of his—the theater—brought a flash of insight to join all three together.

When John goes into the city to see a play he has inordinately poor luck in finding a parking space. Parking garages are usually

The Walking Program

For Keeps:

- Continue walking three or four times a week. Walk 4 miles or 1 hour for each workout.

- Your pace should continue to be brisk—better than 15 minutes per mile if possible.

Notes:

You can time a 4-mile workout in order to measure your pace, or you can time a representative mile within your workout. In the absence of measured miles, use perception of effort as described in Chapter 4.

Now, after Level Four there are no further heights to reach for. You need not increase the distance or time of your workouts. You will probably find, though, that you can better your pace without a great increase in effort. You may soon be gliding through 14-minute miles.

Start to develop a rhythm in your workouts; get a feeling of pace and form. These are the essences of walking that will keep the activity with you. Add them to the best rewards and you can have a partnership with walking that will last for life.

---

full, and he is often forced to drive around for 10 or 15 minutes looking for a space.

Once, he had to park ten blocks away from the theater, and he found himself muttering four-letter epithets. Suddenly, his elementary math flashed on in his brain. Of course—πr^2, the formula for the area of a circle. John visualized the distance from the theater to a parking space as the radius of a circle. Within that circle lay the number of parking spaces potentially available. By parking twice as far as usual from the theater he would not merely double the number of possible spaces, but quadruple them! πr^2.

Walking twice the usual distance from his car to the theater would be easy for John. What is an extra half mile or so when he regularly works out at 4 miles? The extra walking time involved, 6 or 7 minutes, is half the time spent on the search for a closer space.

With a little geometrical help from Euclid, John has changed his philosophy about parking in the city. Now going to the theater is more enjoyable for him than ever.

Good Deeds

Once you have become a strong and graceful walker, you can have as your crowning reward a touch of self-satisfaction. Just find some poor soul who needs your knowledge of walking for fitness. Teach that individual something about form and pace, and point out some of the good reasons for walking. You might save a life by keeping someone who is at medical risk on his or her toes and heels. It is a true act of fellowship, more altruistic than giving money to charity.

References

Barnard, R. James, Glen K. Grimditch, and Jack H. Wilmore. "Physiological Characteristics of Sprint and Endurance Masters Runners." *Medicine and Science in Sports,* vol. 11, no. 2, 1979, pp. 167–71.

Cardus, D., F. Ribas-Cardus, and W. C. McTaggart. "Changes in Blood Viscosity with Exercise Training." *Medicine and Science in Sports and Exercise,* vol. 13, no. 2, 1981, p. 109.

Costill, David L., P. Blom, and L. Hermansen. "Influence of Acute Exercise and Endurance Training on Muscle Glycogen Storage." *Medicine and Science in Sports and Exercise,* vol. 13, no. 2, 1981, p. 90.

Cox, M. H., and Roy J. Shephard. "Employee Fitness, Absenteeism and Job Satisfaction." *Medicine and Science in Sports,* vol. 11, no. 1, 1979, p. 105.

Davies, K. J. A., L. Packer, and G. A. Brooks. "Mitochondrial Biogenesis and Exercise Energetics." *Medicine and Science in Sports and Exercise,* vol. 13, no. 2, 1981, p. 118.

Deshaies, Yves, and Claude Allard. "Serum High-Density Lipoprotein Cholesterol in Male and Female Olympic Athletes." *Medicine and Science in Sports and Exercise,* vol. 14, no. 3, 1982, pp. 207–11.

Faulkner, John A. "Skeletal Muscle—De-Conditioning, Aging and Disease." (Delivered before the American Academy of Physical Medicine and Rehabilitation, Session 4, October 1980).

Fernhall, Bo, Thomas G. Manfredi, and Herman Rierson. "Effects of Ten Weeks of Cardiac Rehabilitation on Blood Clotting and Risk Factors." *The Physician and Sportsmedicine,* February 1984, pp. 85–96.

Higuchi, M., L.-J. Cartier, and John O. Holloszy. "The Effects of Endurance Training on Free Radical Scavenging Enzymes in Rats." *Medicine and Science in Sports and Exercise,* vol. 15, no. 2, 1983, p. 93.

Hoerr, Sharon L. "Exercise: An Alternative to Fad Diets for Adolescent Girls." *The Physician and Sportsmedicine,* February 1984, pp. 76–83.

Holloszy, John O. "Muscle Metabolism during Exercise." (Delivered before the American Academy of Physical Medicine and Rehabilitation, Session 4, October 1980).

———. "Acute Exercise Enhances Glucose Uptake." *The Physician and Sportsmedicine,* February 1983, p. 189.

Jaeger, A. L., T. J. Muckle, and J. D. MacDougall. "The Effect of Exercise on HDL Cholesterol and HDL Apoprotein A." *Medicine and Science in Sports and Exercise,* vol. 15, no. 2, 1983, p. 184.

Kannel, William B., Philip Wolf, Daniel McGee, Thomas R. Dawber, Patricia McNamara, and William P. Castelli. "Systolic Blood Pressure, Arterial Rigidity and Risk of Stroke." *Journal of the American Medical Association,* March 1981, pp. 1225–29.

Lamb, D. R., J. M. Davis, T. Balon, A. C. Snyder, and P. B. Johnson. "Brain 5-Hydroxytryptamine, 5-Hydroxyindoleacetic Acid and Exercise Tolerance." *Medicine and Science in Sports,* vol. 11, no. 1, 1979, pp. 107–8.

Markoff, Richard A., Paul Ryan, and Ted Young. "Endorphins and Mood Changes in Long-Distance Running." *Medicine and Science in Sports and Exercise,* vol. 14, no. 1, 1985, pp. 11–15.

Morgan, William P. "Affective Beneficence of Vigorous Physical Activity." *Medicine and Science in Sports and Exercise,* vol. 17, no. 1, 1985, pp. 94–100.

Murphy, Patrick. "Life Insurers Offer Health Incentives." *The Physician and Sportsmedicine,* March 1984, p. 25.

Oyster, Nancy, Max Morton, and Sheri Linnell. "Physical Activity and Osteoporosis in Post-Menopausal Women." *Medicine and Science in Sports and Exercise,* vol. 16, no. 1, 1984, pp. 44–50.

Pavlou, Konstantin N., Paul A. Levine, Louis C. Fellios, and William P. Steffee. "Cardiac Arrhythmias in Exercised and Non-Exercised Subjects During an 8-Week Weight Reduction Program." *Medicine and Science in Sports and Exercise,* vol. 14, no. 2, 1982, p. 115.

Ransford, Charles P. "A Role for Amines in the Antidepressant Effect of Exercise: A Review." *Medicine and Science in Sports and Exercise,* vol. 14, no. 1, 1982, pp. 1–10.

Sager, Kayleen. "Senior Fitness—for the Health of It." *The Physician and Sportsmedicine,* October 1983, pp. 31–36.

Sheehan, George. "How Important Is the Clock?" *The Physician and Sportsmedicine,* February 1984, p. 47.

———. "Today's Contemplation." *The Physician and Sportsmedicine,* July 1984, p. 37.

Sills, Irene N., and Frank J. Cerny. "Responses to Continuous and Intermittent Exercise in Healthy and Insulin-Dependent Diabetic Children." *Medicine and Science in Sports and Exercise,* vol. 14, no. 6, 1983, pp. 450–54.

Smith, E. L., P. E. Smith, C. P. Ensing, and M. M. Shea. "Exercise in Middle-Aged Women Decreases Bone Involution." *Medicine and Science in Sports and Exercise,* vol. 16, no. 2, 1984, pp. 104–5.

Suominen, Harri, Eino Heikkinen, and Terttu Parkatti. "Effect of Eight Weeks' Physical Training on Muscle and Connective Tissue of the M. Vastus Lateralis in 69-Year-Old Men and Women." *Journal of Gerontology,* vol. 32, 1977, pp. 33–37.

Thorland, William G., and Thomas B. Gilliam. "Comparison of Serum Lipids between Habitually High and Low Active Pre-Adolescent Males." *Medicine and Science in Sports and Exercise,* vol. 13, no. 5, 1981, pp. 316–21.

Webster, W. A., D. P. Smith, J. C. LaRosa, R. Muesing, and P. K. Wilson. "Effects of Twelve Weeks of Jogging on Serum Lipoproteins of Middle-Aged Men." Abstracts of the 25th Annual Meeting of American College of Sports Medicine, vol. 10, no. 1, 1978, p. 55.

Weltman, Arthur, and Bryant Stamford. "Psychological Effects of Exercise." *The Physician and Sportsmedicine,* January 1983, p. 175.

Wirth, A., G. Holm, and Per Bjorntorp. "Effect of Physical Training on Insulin Uptake by the Perfused Rat Liver." *Medicine and Science in Sports and Exercise,* vol. 13, no. 2, 1981, pp. 83–84.

Wright, W. W., Arend Bonen, M. Tan, M. Sopper, D. Hood, and A. N. Belcastro. "Accelerated Glycogen Repletion in Trained Rats." *Medicine and Science in Sports and Exercise,* vol. 13, no. 2, 1981, p. 89.

Young, John R. "Effect of Regular Exercise on Cognition and Personality." *Medicine and Science in Sports,* vol. 10, no. 1, 1978, p. 51.

Chapter 6

Anatomy: Form and Function

Walk, Don't Run, Down the Road to Fitness

In the 1920s and 1930s, there was a widely held theory of life that advised against strenuous activity. Sports that were moderately to severely stressful would wear out your tissues and organs and you would become old before your time.

"Never run when you can walk. Never walk when you can stand still. Never stand when you can sit," advised the theory makers.

The concept is quickly discredited when the engineering of the human body is examined. A look at the human skeleton reveals a figure made of curves, both subtle and more defined. There is the S-shaped curve of the spine, the turn of the femur just below the ball and socket joint of the hip, and the arch of the foot. The curves contribute to the structural essence of a weight bearing, weight moving skeleton. A straight, rigid skeleton would bear weight well, but would be immobile. A skeleton with curves and hinges is designed for movement.

The rigging of skeletal muscles and their attachments to the various bones confirms that skeletal form is integral with function.

- The supple spine yields at each step with the left/right movements of the shoulders and pelvis.

- The hingelike knee joint keeps a straight forward line of stride.

- The flexibility of the ankle allows the foot to accommodate to an uneven terrain.

- The springlike arch of the foot cushions each footstep and relieves the pressure on the knee and hip joints.

The sizes and shapes of the bones and how they are connected to each other allow for many types of movements, both extreme and gentle. The extreme motions, as in gymnastics, can be sustained for only a matter of minutes. The gentle motions, as those of walking, can be continued for hours.

But wouldn't the bones and joints last longer by not moving at all, as in standing or sitting? The question is a logical one but it does not take into account the fact that bare bones do not move themselves around like a Halloween skeleton. Muscles move bones. Muscle fibers contract and relax. That is all they do. There is, of course, a complex biochemical process involved, but functionally it is contraction and relaxation.

A muscle fiber can also contract and hold the contraction, though not for long. Fatigue sets in quickly when a muscle fiber is kept in a state of contraction. Muscle fibers much prefer to contract and relax in a continuous cycle rather than remain in tension.

Let's apply this muscle fiber axiom to actual activities. We can start with the old axiom, "Never run when you can walk, and never walk when you can stand still."

Only Statues Stand

In running and walking, there are many muscle groups involved in alternate contraction and relaxation. At the instant that some are contracting, others are relaxing. No muscle group has to sustain a prolonged contraction.

In standing, the muscles do not contract as vigorously, but they keep a certain amount of constant contractile tone. Thus, the muscles do not get a chance to relax between contractions. When you stand, your body is held upright by a balanced tension of the muscles of the right and left sides. The legs are held straight by the opposing muscles of the thigh—the quadriceps and the hamstrings. If this constant and equally balanced muscle act were not performed well you would lurch to one side. If the balanced muscles suddenly went from tension to relaxation you would collapse under your own weight.

The constant muscle tension required of standing is not to the body's liking. That is intuitive as well as scientific knowledge. Just estimate how long you can stand stark still without any movement. Even trained honor guards standing at attention for an hour or more cannot stand entirely still. They wiggle their toes from time to time and alternately tense and release the muscles of the leg.

There is another important reason why the body won't stand for standing still. (You see, the physiologic truth has even crept into our language as an idiom.) The reason is one of hydraulic engineering. The heart, when it pumps blood down to the toes, expects to get the blood back so it can send it to the lungs for a fresh oxygen supply. The blood returns from the toes via the veins of the legs, and if you are standing, it is a vertical uphill run. The blood pressure of the veins is barely able to counter the force of gravity over the 3- to 4-foot distance from the toes to the heart. When you are standing, the legs become heavy with blood that is collecting more and more carbon dioxide and lactic acid. No wonder it is difficult to stand still for any length of time.

Chairmanship

Compared to standing, sitting is not quite so out of tune with the design of the musculoskeletal system. The blood returning from the legs to the heart does not have as steep an uphill journey. The muscles of the legs are more relaxed though the muscles of the upper body are probably more tense than in standing. You know how stiff your body can feel after sitting at a desk in a low-backed chair for an hour or two. You know how your joints practically creak when you get out of a car after a long trip.

I can go along with "Never stand when you can sit," but I'd rather that neither sitting nor standing be endurance events. Even if the never-never theory calls for walking at one stage ("never run when you can walk"), it is a negative call, and walking has enough advantages and gifts that it should be adopted for positive reasons.

On the Move—Walking

We can walk for a couple of hours or more if the pace is not too intense. It is an indication of how our bodies work best.

In walking, muscles are not kept under constant tension. With each left-right sequence of muscles contract once and relax once. There is, of course, precise coordination of the muscles in pairs: muscle A contracts while muscle B relaxes. This reciprocal action is multiplied by more muscles than there are letters in the alphabet.

This repeated contraction-relaxation sequence of each of the leg muscles not only moves the body horizontally, but it moves the blood vertically within the veins of the legs. The muscles actually act as a pump to send blood from the legs toward the heart, thus improving circulation in the legs and making more blood available for the heart to pump out to the rest of the body.

Walking works. Never stand when you can walk.

On the Move—Running

If the motions of walking are better than standing, why not go one step further to running? One reason is that running, unlike walking, causes injuries. The injury rate is unacceptably high, close to 50 percent in some of the broad studies. Running injuries are not only numerous, but varied. Runners suffer shin splints, metatarsal sprains, pulled hamstrings, upper and lower back injuries, knee ligament tears, and even stress fractures.

It is no wonder. Running generates extreme vertical forces, up to four times your body weight at each footstep. The bones, joints, and ligaments can withstand such jolting for only a short time. A 7,000- to 8,000-stride workout (approximately 10 kilometers, or 6 miles) is risky. A *walker's* musculoskeletal system, in contrast, must withstand a maximum of only one and a half times body weight at each stride. Walkers can travel long distances, and injuries are rare.

The traumatic injuries of running just mentioned are painful and disabling. There are other injuries that runners may suffer unknowingly.

Herman L. Falsetti, M.D., and his co-workers at the University of Iowa observed significant blood changes in runners after road races. They found red-blood-cell destruction and lowered hemoglobin values that resulted in lower oxygen-carrying capacity. The investigators were able to track down the cause to the repeated pounding that occurs with running.

There have been no studies of walkers to check out red-blood-cell destruction, but it seems unlikely that walking, graceful and unpounding, would cause that trouble.

Never run when you can walk.

Jogging the Sex Drive

Exercise affects the function of practically every organ in the body from bone structure to blood chemistry to brain electrical activity.

Why shouldn't it influence sex as well? Of course it should, and it does.

Several studies of men have shown that moderate endurance exericse—cycling, running, walking—increases testosterone levels. Very severe and/or prolonged exercise decreases testosterone levels, sometimes to exceptionally low levels.

Studies of women have shown sex hormone cycle abnormalities and lack of ovulation when there is extensive exercise training.

The results of these studies started to appear in the medical literature in the 1970s, but competitive athletes knew about them long before. Male runners training at 40 or more miles per week in preparation for a major road race experience a diminished sex drive. Menses cease in women training at the same distances.

Running for fitness may start out as a moderate endurance sport, but being competitive creatures to a greater or lesser extent we are too easily drawn to longer distances and a faster pace. Hormone levels then become depressed, and both male and female runners edge closer to unisex central.

Walking, in contrast, runs no such risk. Walking is a *moderate* exercise and increases sexual hormone production.

In the Beginning

When we research mankind's evolutionary heritage we can understand why walking is so natural to us today. Early man lived a life of hunting and gathering. Much of his time was spent in walking, sometimes over long distances.

There was not much running except for short bursts—to escape from danger or to chase after a small, slow animal. Man is actually among the slowest of all animals. Most animals our size can run 25 to 45 mph on the open plains. The best world-class sprinters can barely do 23 mph on an artificial track made for speed. Early man, looking for his dinner, could not hope to run down an animal over 200 yards of uneven terrain. Yet he could track the animal for several hours or even a full day at a walk. A ten-dinner game animal—a deer or wildebeest, for instance—could be worn out over a period of 12 hours.

Primitive man also walked from place to place gathering roots from the ground and fruit from trees. Seasonal migrations necessitated walking great distances. Those individuals who had good walking stamina survived to pass the trait on to their offspring. It is those hominid to *Homo sapiens* muscles and bones, grown strong for walking over many millennia, that we have inherited. Distance running is not in our bones and joints and muscles. Walking is.

Go with your genes.

All the evidence from the study of anatomy, physiology, evolution, and sports medicine leaves no choice but walking as *the* exercise for *Homo sapiens.* Let gazelles leap; let greyhounds run; let silkworms spin (and cycle). Man is made to walk. It's time to get in step with our bodies.

References

Bonen, Arend, and Hans K. Keizer. "Athletic Menstrual Cycle Irregularity: Endocrine Response to Exercise and Training." *The Physician and Sportsmedicine,* August 1984, pp. 78–94.

Bullen, Beverly A., Gary S. Skrinar, Inese Z. Beitins, Gretchen vonMering, Barry A. Turnbull, and Janet W. McArthur. "Induction of Menstrual Disorders by Strenuous Exercise in Untrained Women." *The New England Journal of Medicine,* vol. 312, no. 21, 1985, pp. 1349–53.

Cunningham, L. N., C. Labrie, J. S. Soeldner, R. E. Gleason, and N. Anderson. "Aging and Running Related to Peripheral Blood Flow." *Medicine and Science in Sports and Exercise,* vol. 14, no. 2, 1982, p. 165.

Dressendorfer, Rudolph H., and Charles E. Wade. "The Muscular Overuse Syndrome in Long-Distance Runners." *The Physician and Sportsmedicine,* November 1983, pp. 116–30.

Falsetti, Herman L., Edmund R. Burke, Ronald D. Feld, Edward C. Frederick, and Cam Ratering. "Hematological Variations after Endurance Running with Hard- and Soft-Soled Running Shoes." *The Physician and Sportsmedicine,* August 1983, pp. 118–27.

Fellingham, Gilbert W., Elmo S. Roundy, A. Garth Fisher, and G. Rex Bryce. "Caloric Cost of Walking and Running." *Medicine and Science in Sports and Exercise,* vol. 10, no. 2, 1978, pp. 132–36.

Grant, J. C. Boileau. *Grant's Atlas of Anatomy.* 5th ed. Baltimore: Williams and Wilkins Co., 1962.

Holloszy, John O. "Muscle Metabolism during Exercise." (Delivered before the American Academy of Physical Medicine and Rehabilitation, Session 4, October 1980).

McConnell, Timothy R., and Wayne E. Sinning. "Exercise and Temperature Effects on Human Sperm Production and Testosterone Levels." *Medicine and Science in Sports and Exercise,* vol. 16, no. 1, 1984, pp. 51–55.

Massicotte, D. R., G. Avon, and M. Portmann. "Cardiovascular Responses to Cycling and Walking or Running." *Medicine and Science in Sports and Exercise,* vol. 15, no. 2, 1983, p. 111.

Smith, J. L., Rudolph H. Dressendorfer, and E. A. Amsterdam. "Evaluation of a Walking Program for Patients with Ischemic Heart Disease." *Medicine and Science in Sports,* vol. 11, no. 1, 1979, p. 100.

Vogel, Robert B., Cindy A. Books, Catherine Ketchum, Christian W. Zauner, and Frederick T. Murray. "Increase of Free and Total Testosterone during Submaximal Exercise in Normal Males." *Medicine and Science in Sports and Exercise,* vol. 17, no. 1, 1985, pp. 119–23.

Wakat, Diane K., Kathleen A. Sweeney, and Alan D. Rogol. "Reproductive System Function in Women Cross-Country Runners." *Medicine and Science in Sports and Exercise,* vol. 14, no. 4, 1982, pp. 263–69.

Chapter 7

Safekeeping

Health without Harm

My personal physician, Dr. J. George Melnick, has a special interest in pain syndromes. He has treated many patients whose painful conditions were unrelieved by medication. These cases often involved the muscles and/or joints. George tells me that his practice has increased sharply since the running revolution gained momentum in the 1970s. Many of his new patients come in with back problems, foot injuries, spasms of assorted muscles from head to toe, bone bruises, and/or acute inflammation of one or more joints. He often advises them that exercise is dangerous to their health.

Another physician, Douglas M. Levin, M.D., is of a similar opinion. In a letter to the editor of the *New York Times* he says, "... from personal experience in running, rowing, swimming, bicycling, and vigorous racket sports, I can vouch for the destructive potential of all of them."

How ironic that sports and exercise, heralded as promoters of fitness and health, cause injury instead.

By taking a look at the hazards of other sports and exercise activities, you will find that walking is the safest exercise and you will learn how to avoid even its minimal dangers.

Other Sports May Be Harmful to Your Health

Sports by their very nature:

- make the muscles work hard
- place great pressures on joints, ligaments, and tendons
- influence the metabolic processes of the body
- place the athlete at risk during workouts in hot weather, cold weather, and conditions of high humidity

In almost every sport the athelete is liable to injury. The evidence is firm, not just anecdotal. It is based on good studies and well-documented case reports appearing in the sports medicine literature. A sampler from such journals as *Medicine and Science in Sports and Exercise, The Physician and Sportsmedicine, Journal of Applied Physiology,* and *International Journal of Sports Medicine* may raise your eyebrows.

Injuries are expected—and occur aplenty—in contact sports where blows are exchanged (boxing), where blocking and tackling take place (football and rugby), and where the opponent is forced into a compromised position (wrestling). The rules of these all-out contact sports allow for more force than many bodies (and heads) can handle.

In ice hockey, the injury rate is high, but most of the injuries are not serious. In soccer, the injury rate is lower, but still frequent. The equestrian sports have their fair share of injuries, particularly when the injuries from fox hunting and polo are added to the tally.

Off-season sports are not without their dangers. According to a California study of varsity athletes, basketball was involved most in off-season injuries. One reason was that most athletes chose basketball as their second sport, but another reason was that basketball places great forces on the ankles, knees, and back.

Walking was not even listed among all the sports for keeping in shape between competitive seasons. A little remediation is in order.

Volleyball, the sport that is supposedly gentle enough to be played by mixed teams at picnics, can be vigorous and intense. Fingers, ankles, and knees are most vulnerable.

Aerobic dancing, safe and easy according to its promoters, has attracted millions of adherents. It has also caused an alarming number of injuries. Consider the study by Douglas H. Richie, Jr., D.P.M., and his colleagues, which showed that among 1,233 students in aerobic dance classes for an average time of six months each, over 40 percent had been injured. The investigators also surveyed 58 instructors, each with an average time of participation of 30 months. Seventy-five percent of the instructors had been injured at least once.

Frequency and injury rate are directly related in such studies. If the participant attended more than four classes a week, the injury rate was significantly higher. Is there any exercise that is truly safe to pursue?

The Pedestrian Sports

Walking is the beacon of light in the fitness gloom. None of the injuries common to any of the sports from boxing to aerobic dancing is seen in walking. Walking is inherently safe if ordinary care is taken. But rare as they are, walking injuries are possible and precautions are worthwhile.

A little knowledge of running injuries will go a long way toward preparing one to avoid any hazards in walking. The same preventive measures apply.

Many of the running injuries—muscle pulls, joint trauma, bone bruises, ligament and tendon tears, and stress fractures—are classified as the "too" injuries—too fast, too far, too frequent, too sudden. To avoid these acute injuries, the following precautions are essential:

- Increase distance and speed gradually over several weeks.
- Warm up before working out.
- Workouts should be moderate in distance and intensity.
- Workouts should be no more than four times a week.
- After working out, cool down slowly.
- Stretch afterward.
- If injured, rest.

There are three other "too" injuries as well. They involve physiological forces rather than the physical rending of tissue:

1. The Unnatural Muscle Contraction of Downhill Running

   In downhill running the eccentric contraction of muscles (the forced lengthening of a muscle as it tries to contract) can cause muscle fiber damage. Normally, a muscle shortens as it contracts. For example, when you rise from a half knee bend to a standing position the quadriceps muscle group contracts and shortens to straighten the leg. In downhill running, the weight of the body causes the leg to bend with the foot strike of each stride. Thus, the quads lengthen as they tense to support the body's weight. It is not in the design of the muscle fibers to lengthen with strong contraction. The muscles will let you know about it.

A few years ago, I went on a day trip to Baxter State Park to climb Mount Katahdin, the highest peak in Maine. The Abol Trail for the most part is easy uphill hiking with a few scrambles mixed in, but the total distance is respectable. I was in good condition and the climb to the summit was not tiring. After lunch at the top, I started down. I thought to myself, "The climb up caused hardly any stress. Now I can let gravity carry me down with no effort at all."

It was not more than a couple of miles when I began to feel a soreness in my thighs. "Strange," I thought. "Maybe it's just a little muscle tightness that will ease out if I slow down a bit."

As the miles went on the soreness became pain, and the pain turned from worse to frightening. By the time I reached the base of the trail I felt crippled from the waist down. I could not imagine what was happening to me. Perhaps the great spirit, Pamola, who the Abenaki Indians say still lives in the mountain, had visited a curse upon a walker who thought the climb to the top was easy. Perhaps it was some dread virus striking at muscles sensitized by hiking.

No, it turned out to be the eccentric muscle contraction of downhill walking. It was 48 hours before the pain eased somewhat, and it was a week until I could run across a street.

What can you do to prevent this type of injury? There are two choices: (1) abstinence from downhill walking and (2) mild to moderate downhill training in preparation for any long downhill trek. An ounce of prevention. . . .

2. Muscle Fiber Destruction in Marathons and Other Ultradistance Races

Muscle injury can occur on the flat as well as downhill. All it takes is distance. Several studies of marathoners have reported evidence of muscle fiber damage. Blood analysis of marathon runners 24 hours after the race has shown extremely high levels of creatine kinase, an enzyme marker of muscle cell destruction. Leg muscle biopsies of marathoners provided microscopic pictures of cell death of muscle fibers and acute inflammatory changes in adjacent tissue areas.

Herbert L. Fred, M.D., a 49-year-old physician, has reported his personal reflections on running a 100-mile ultramarathon. He had taken aspirin before and during the race in order to quiet down some of the pain of tendinitis at the knee. Otherwise, he took only fluids (tea flavored with honey and lime, half-strength ERG, and bouillon).

At 70 miles, he noticed such mental changes as irritability, a startled reaction to noise, and resentment toward other runners using the track.

At 92 miles, heat illness struck. His skin was pale and clammy; he was extremely nauseated; and he became dizzy. His helpers had him lie down and urged him to take more fluids. After 15 minutes of rest and cool towels, he continued and finished in 22:21:39, almost a full day's work. After crossing the finish line, he felt an overall numbness—more mental than physical—and he had an image of himself as being small and insignificant, a far cry from the pride he expected to feel.

Dr. Fred did not undergo any specific testing for muscle damage but he reports that his "thighs shrank considerably." That, too, is a sign of tissue destruction.

No studies have been done on the race-walkers who compete in marathons, but it is likely that they, too, suffer the muscle injury of distance.

At what distance does the muscle breakdown begin? That varies with the individual, level of fitness, and speed of walking. It is probably somewhere between 8 and 15 miles. For safekeeping, you should keep to less than your own critical mileage. Or, if you must complete a longer distance for a special reason, the pace should not be pressed as in a race.

For my old bones the critical distance is about 10 miles at a very fast pace. I have had no post-workout soreness at 5 km. (3.1 miles) or 10 km. (6.2 miles), but 10 miles brings on a weariness of the legs and a little muscle tenderness through the following day. I have done only two competitive walks of 10 miles, and the second confirmed the wisdom I should have learned from the first: when your ego gives poor advice, listen to your body. Nowadays I do no more than 6.2 miles in competition unless it's a blue moon event of special importance.

You will know when you have gone beyond your own critical mileage. If the muscles are not quite recovered 48 hours after a far or furious walk, your body is saying, "You missed a rest stop somewhere back on the road to fitness."

3. Depression and Other Harmful Effects of Overtraining

You must exercise mileage care in individual workouts, and you must watch for weekly and monthly totals that add up to too much. Overtraining is seen with fair frequency in runners. Some become "obligatory" runners, working out at more than 8 miles a day, more than four days a week.

In a recent round table symposium published in *The Physician and Sportsmedicine,* it was brought out that many of the signs and symptoms of mental depression are seen with overtraining: loss of motivation, insomnia, anorexia, "the blues." This physiological state of exhaustion brought other unpleasantness, including chronic muscle soreness, decrease in immune response, potassium depletion, increased resting heart rate, and a slower return of heart rate to normal after a brief exercise effort. Part of the process is an exhaustion of the endocrines, especially the master gland of the system, the pituitary.

Women know more accurately than men when overtraining threatens. At 40 or more miles per week, ovulation may cease and the menstrual cycle be disrupted.

For both women and men of less than elite caliber, 40 to 50 miles per week seems to be the danger point of overtraining. Frequent competition included in that total mileage hastens the pathology.

Although there has been no report of overtraining in walkers, I have noticed a little crankiness in a couple of race-walking friends who put in high mileage.

The precautions are easy enough:

- Allow enough rest time between workouts, ideally 48 hours.
- Have an occasional change in your workout routine—different routes and different distances.
- If you enter races, avoid incessant competition.
- Remember that high-mileage achievements do not equal more fitness and health than workouts at 4 miles, 4 mph, and four times a week.

Overtraining is a serious pathological state, and recovery may take up to three months. Cure involves abstinence from workouts for two or three weeks and then only very light workouts for a month or more. An ounce of prevention is better.

Blisters and "Black Toenails"

There are two injuries that walkers do suffer. The first is blisters, and the second is "black toenails." They are seen with fair frequency in walkers who have reached fitness levels but still need work on form.

Runners also suffer these minor injuries, but I think they are ashamed to admit to them. A runner can properly miss a few workouts because of a hamstring muscle pull or Achilles tendinitis. But blisters?

Nevertheless, the toes need attention. Blisters are caused by repeated friction of the bottoms of the toes. (Less frequently, they may occur on the ball of the foot.)

Blisters are prevented by a swipe of petroleum jelly on the undersurfaces of the toes and by wearing a pair of thin socks (cotton, silk, or polypropylene) inside of your athletic socks.

"Black toenail" is caused by too much pressure from the front of the shoe, strike after stride. Bleeding occurs in the nail bed and the nail turns black and blue (mostly black).

This injury is preventable by clipping the nails short and rounding them with an emery board. For a final touch, a little petroleum jelly is used on and around the nails. Then, too, your walking shoes should be long enough in the toe portion that you do not jam the toenails against the front of the shoe at each step. The shoes should be snug around the arch, instep, and heel so the entire foot does not slide forward.

It is better to prevent "black toenail" than to have to cure it. The black color lasts for weeks, long after the soreness is gone. The cure involves keeping the toes clean, keeping pressure off the toenails, and waiting out the time it takes for the nail to grow out. If you are a woman, you can cover the nail with red nail polish.

An Environment of Conspiracy

Many folks go to the beach on a sunny, hot day and take in the rays for a few hours. There is a small chance of heatstroke.

Take the same people, change their swimsuits into running shorts and T-shirts, and shout, "The last one to the finish line is ugly." If the finish line is an hour away, heatstroke will surely play a part in the event.

Heat is but one environmental agent that walkers have to watch. There is also humidity, pollution, cold, and pollen for the allergic. Walkers are often at equal risk with runners and other athletes, and it is only knowledge that will keep danger at bay.

Some Like It Hot

A couple of years ago I was in a walking race where the temperature was in the upper eighties. It was not a long race, only 5 km., but a half hour in the blistering sun slowed my pace almost a minute per mile. Every quarter mile, I sponged cold water onto my face and head, but it brought only minor relief.

Within the first mile, one of the women walkers, Roberta B., passed me and never let up for the rest of the race. Her time for the 5 km. was a personal best. Roberta likes it hot.

Most walkers would be prudent to figure otherwise for themselves. Roger W. Hubbard of the Army Research Institute of Environmental Medicine advises that exercise lowers the critical threshold for heatstroke. He cites animal study parallels that show that exhaustive exercise can make an individual more than ten times as susceptible to heatstroke.

Dr. George Sheehan agrees. He feels that the greatest danger to athletes is heat, and he suggests that as summer advances, early morning exercise is the best way to avoid the heat. Then in his usual eloquence, Dr. Sheehan tells us, "It is not heat that kills . . . it is ignorance."

A fascinating small side note to exercising in a hot environment is the balancing of (1) the absorption of radiant heat from the sun and (2) the evaporation of sweat from the skin to cool the body. Should you be more concerned about reflecting the hot sun or facilitating the evaporation of perspiration? If the sun is bright, worry about the sun and wear a white T-shirt. If it is hot and cloudy, a mesh shirt will provide better cooling through evaporation.

The use of sunscreen presents a similar dilemma. Sunscreen blocks the ultraviolet rays but retards the evaporation of perspiration. Apply the shirt principle.

Jack Frost Can Shiver Your Timbers

If there is one realm of risk more perilous for walkers than for runners, it is working out in cold weather. A runner can complete a good 4 miles in a half hour or so. A walker on the same course would have to spend an extra 10 to 20 minutes in the cold.

If weather conditions are very cold, cold and wet, or cold and windy, body heat can be lost rapidly. Walkers must take precautions to prevent hypothermia.

I remember one New York Marathon that took place on a cool, drizzly October Sunday. I was sitting in the press section at the finish line, holding an umbrella to keep my note pad dry. I was covering a race within a race—the hundred or so competitors who chose not to run but to walk. These walkers were testing their mettle not only against distance and time but also against the elements. The first walker to finish was Bo Gustaffson of Sweden, whose time was 3 hours and 19 plus minutes. In contrast, runner Rod Dixon from New Zealand crossed the finish line in 2 hours and 9 minutes. That extra hour and 10 minutes in the cold, wet, outdoors takes a good deal of heat from the body, sometimes more than the body generates in movement.

Behind Gustaffson were walkers Marco Evoniuk (United States), Raul Gonzales (Mexico), and only three others in less than 4 hours. Most of the less illustrious, though competent, walkers came through in 5 hours, give or take 20 minutes.

Bob F. was in this second group. He is lean and has little natural insulation to protect him against 5 hours of heat loss. After crossing the finish line and having his number recorded, Bob turned pale and clammy and began to shiver uncontrollably. Two fellow walkers who had a little more reserve on their bones saw him and were alarmed. They quickly decided that their own body heat was the handiest source of warmth.

After 10 minutes of hug-a-bunch therapy, Bob's shivering relented and his color returned. He recovered well, but for a little while it was a close race with Jack Frost.

Cold weather can lower your total body heat reserve, and it can find particular points of weakness to attack. The lungs are prime targets. Cold air is heated as you breathe in, and the tissues of the respiratory tract become cooled by the air as it passes in contact with them. This heat exchange normally occurs in the upper levels of the respiratory tract.

During cold weather exercise, when breathing is faster and deeper, the heat exchange level moves deeper into the respiratory tree. Along with the heat exchange there is an increased loss of water vapor from the lungs. The result may be bronchospasm and asthma.

The precautions are as they always have been:

- Don't exercise in extremely cold weather.

- If the weather is just very cold, don't exercise too vigorously.

- Wear a cold weather mask if the air is very cold and dry.

And a more modern precaution:

- If you are asthmatic to begin with and use medication occasionally, take the medication prophylactically before exercising in the cold.

Cold does not always appear in blizzard white to shiver your timbers. A pleasant autumn day with mild temperatures can be more guileful than a subfreezing day in January. Here's a scenario for you:

You are doing a workout with your walking club. The day is cloudy, the temperature is in the midfifties. You are wearing shorts and a T-shirt—enough cover for a vigorous 5 km. You finish the distance behind the really fast walkers but well ahead of the slower ones. Respectable.

You have worked up a good sweat and are waiting for everyone to finish so a promised relay race can be organized. More than an hour passes. There is a little breeze and your sweat-soaked T-shirt is starting to feel a little cold. Your warm-up suit is in your car a couple of blocks away; but the relay teams are being chosen and the race is soon to start.

You are to be the anchor of one of the two teams, and that means another 15 or 20 minutes of standing around. The race starts and you are becoming more chilled. So far you are experiencing only shivering and none of the more serious signs of hypothermia.

Finally the teammate who is to pass the baton to you is approaching. He is even with his rival. As the two batons are handed off simultaneously, you feel a sense of excitement that this is going to be a close race. You both go out quickly and match strides for most of the quarter-mile distance. You feel a glow of warmth and realize that you have forgotten about being cold.

About 50 yards from the finish line, your legs become a little wobbly and you are forced to slow down. Your competitor crosses the finish line a couple of seconds before you. Perhaps it was the heat loss before the race.

An unlikely scenario? Not at all. It is exactly what happened to me a couple of years ago. You may be sure that a couple of minutes after the race I was zipped into a warm-up suit. It was a good lesson.

Cold weather conditions that are less than extreme need not keep you from your regular workouts. Just select the right outfit, keep a good measure of common sense about you, and off you go. Here is some cool counsel:

- Woolen clothing is warm, though itchy. A silk or polypropylene layer is better against the skin. All breathe well and will help get rid of perspiration. The outermost layer can be nylon or Gore-Tex to keep the wind on the outside. Turtlenecks and long johns add to comfort in the cold as do mittens and a hat.

- The initial shock of stepping out into the cold can be softened by an indoor warm-up.

- Another secret to preserving heat is to do the first part of your workout against the wind so that the last part will be with the wind. A 5½-mph breeze, not too fierce in itself, added to a 4½-mph walking speed equals windy. It's better to face that adversary when you are fresh and not yet sweaty. On your return your tired muscles will have a 1-mph following wind, and the entire workout will not leave you resentful about the price of fitness.

The Pollution Solution

I have seen a number of cars with bumper stickers that urge other drivers to share the road with a runner. That is all fine and brotherly, but there is an inequity in their relative contributions to the atmosphere that they share. The runners take in oxygen and exhale carbon dioxide. The cars take in oxygen and spew out carbon monoxide.

Carbon monoxide from the exhausts of cars can affect athletes' performances. Carbon monoxide binds with hemoglobin just as oxygen does, except the affinity of carbon monoxide for hemoglobin is over 100 times that of oxygen.

Carbon monoxide levels in the blood, as measured by the percentage of carboxyhemoglobin, increase markedly when you just stand around near auto traffic. If you exercise near traffic, the carboxyhemoglobin levels rise even higher because of the greater volume of polluted air inhaled per minute.

Because carbon monoxide exposure sharply increases the risk of cardiovascular morbidity and mortality, exercising near auto traffic might cancel out the major benefits of fitness training. If that is not enough reason, you might also note that carbon monoxide binds to myoglobin (the oxygen-carrying molecule of muscle), thus reducing your performance ability.

Safety First to Last

Runners and walkers are just as open to physical assault as anyone else who frequents the parks, streets, and other public places.

Athletes are targets of not only two-legged creatures, but also of dogs and pigeons flying overhead. Then there are the creatures in wheeled vehicles.

There are standard precautions that you can take for safety in each case. For time and place of greater than usual risk, a few imaginative ways and means are at the ready.

Sharing Should Be Voluntary

If you are to have company while walking, you choose who it will be. No surprises, thank you! Play it safe.

- There is safety in numbers. Group workouts discourage pillage and especially deter rape.

- Walk in open areas where concealment is difficult.

- Select a route so that the last part of your workout, when you are most tired, is the safest.

- Do not wear or carry valuables openly.

- Be aware. Do not let the rhythm of your walking put you into a trance.

- Keep an inviolate personal space around you at all times. If anyone comes close to your personal space, warn him off with a loud, "Get away from me!" Do not be embarrassed that you may have insulted an innocent person. It is he who should be embarrassed to have come so close that he alarmed you.

- Look confident, and look aware.

Dealing with Wheels

Be on guard on a road where vehicles travel. No one cares more about your safety than you do.

- Walk against traffic when possible.

- Trust no driver. Presume that drivers are at best incompetent and at worst homicidal.

- Avoid workout routes where there is no place to step quickly off the road to safety.

- Consider wearing an outlandish outfit. If cars slow down out of curiosity rather than caution, at least they have slowed down.

Keeping Hounds at Bay

Dogs are usually man's best friend, but you might encounter an exception. Here are some tips on how to handle the situation.

- Shout at the dog.

- Bark back.

- Throw a rock or, better still, a handful of gravel near the dog.

- Ignore the dog if you judge it to be unlikely to bite, and just keep on walking.

Cat Calls

Nonathletes with little maturity, class, and grace may offer expressions of ridicule. Select an appropriate response from the following, or devise your own rejoinder.

- "Yo, baby—this is an Olympic sport. So bug off."

- "Yeah, you just try and keep up with me."

- "Sir, you are ignorant and uncouth."

- "Madam, you are ill-bred and odious."

- "Barbarian."

Once, a woman in a passing car called out to me, "Don't you know that jogging is bad for your sex drive?"

I replied without missing a stride, "But this is walking, and walking's an aphrodisiac."

She slowed down as if to stop and said (in jest, I think), "It is? Hey wait for me!"

Walking's dangers are generally fewer than in other sports, and you should be pleased with yourself for having chosen the safest exercise. With knowledge, awareness, and a few basic precautions, walking will bring you health without harm.

References

Bernhang, Arthur M., and Georgine Winslett. "Equestrian Injuries." *The Physician and Sportsmedicine,* January 1983, pp. 90–97.

Bixby-Hammett, Doris M. "Head Injuries in the Equestrian Sports." *The Physician and Sportsmedicine,* August 1983, pp. 82–86.

Brown, Richard L., Edward C. Frederick, Herman L. Falsetti, Edmund R. Burke, and Allan J. Ryan. "Overtraining of Athletes—A Round Table." *The Physician and Sportsmedicine,* June 1983, pp. 92–110.

Dressendorfer, Rudolph H., and Charles E. Wade. "The Muscular Overuse Syndrome in Long-Distance Runners." *The Physician and Sportsmedicine,* November 1983, pp. 116–30.

Ende, Leigh S., and Jack Wickstrom. "Ballet Injuries." *The Physician and Sportsmedicine,* July 1982, pp. 100–118.

Estwanik, Joseph, and George D. Rovere. "Wrestling Injuries in North Carolina High Schools." *The Physician and Sportsmedicine,* January 1983, pp. 100–108.

Evenson, Laura. "Parachuting: High Risk in Free-Flying Sport." *The Physician and Sportsmedicine,* October 1983, pp. 171–74.

Falsetti, Herman L., Edmund R. Burke, Ronald D. Feld, Edward C. Frederick, and Cam Ratering. "Hematological Variations after Endurance Running with Hard- and Soft-Soled Running Shoes." *The Physician and Sportsmedicine,* August 1983, pp. 118–27.

Fred, Herbert L. "Reflections on a 100-Mile Run: Effects of Aspirin Therapy." *Medicine and Science in Sports and Exercise,* vol. 12, no. 3, 1980, pp. 212–15.

Gangitano, R., A. Pulvirenti, and S. Ardito. "Volley-ball Injuries: Clinical and Statistical Findings." *Italian Journal of Sports Traumatology,* vol. 3, no. 1, 1981, pp. 31–44.

Glanzer, JoLynn, and Martin Richards. "Chronic Subdural Hematoma in a Wrestler." *The Physician and Sportsmedicine,* February 1984, pp. 121–22.

Griffin, Rick, Keith Peterson, and John R. Halseth. "Injuries in Professional Rodeo." *The Physician and Sportsmedicine,* August 1983, pp. 110–16.

Gunderson, H. M., J. A. Parliman, and J. A. Parker. "Changes in Specific Serum Constituents Associated with Muscle Damage in Marathon Runners." *Medicine and Science in Sports and Exercise,* vol. 14, no. 2, 1982, p. 172.

Hagerman, F. C., R. S. Hikida, R. S. Staron, W. M. Sherman, and David L. Costill. "Muscle Fiber Necrosis in Marathon Runners." *Medicine and Science in Sports and Exercise,* vol. 15, no. 2, 1983, p. 164.

Harrison, C. Scott. "Fox Hunting Injuries in North America." *The Physician and Sportsmedicine,* October 1984, pp. 130–37.

Hubbard, Roger W. "Effects of Exercise in the Heat on Predisposition to Heat Stroke." *Medicine and Science in Sports,* vol. 11, no. 1, 1979, pp. 66–71.

Itin, P., A. Haenel, and H. Stalder. Letter to the Editor. *The New England Journal of Medicine,* vol. 311, no. 26, 1984, p. 1703.

Jacobs, I. "Effects of Thermal Dehydration on Performance of the Wingate Anaerobic Test." *International Journal of Sports Medicine,* vol. 1, no. 1, 1980, pp. 21–24.

Jaeger, A. L., T. J. Muckle, and J. D. MacDougall. "The Effect of Exercise on HDL Cholesterol and HDL Apoprotein A." *Medicine and Science in Sports and Exercise,* vol. 15, no. 2, 1983, p. 184.

Jenkins, R. R., D. Martin, and E. Goldberg. "Lipid Peroxidation in Skeletal Muscle during Atrophy and Acute Exercise." *Medicine and Science in Sports and Exercise,* vol. 15, no. 2, 1983, p. 93.

McCarroll, John R., Craig Meaney, and Jon M. Sieber. "Profile of Youth Soccer Injuries." *The Physician and Sportsmedicine,* February 1984, pp. 113–17.

Mueller, Frederick O., and Carl S. Blyth. "Annual Survey of Catastrophic Football Injuries: 1977–1983." *The Physician and Sportsmedicine,* March 1985, pp. 75–81.

Nicholson, John P., and David B. Case. "Carboxyhemoglobin Levels in New York City Runners." *The Physician and Sportsmedicine,* March 1983, pp. 135–38.

———. "Cheerleaders Suffer Few Serious Injuries." *The Physician and Sportsmedicine,* January 1983, pp. 25–26.

Richie, Douglas H., Jr., Steven Kelso, and Patricia A. Bellucci. "Aerobic Dance Injuries: A Retrospective Study of Instructors and Participants." *The Physician and Sportsmedicine,* February 1985, pp. 130–40.

Rogers, Cindy Christian. "Firing Up for Fitness." *The Physician and Sportsmedicine,* April 1984, pp. 134–42.

Rose, Clifton P., and Dan Bailey. "Injuries to Athletes Outside Their NCAA Sports." *The Physician and Sportsmedicine,* September 1983, pp. 102–5.

Rosegrant, Susan. "Women's Rugby: Conditioning Reduces Injuries." *The Physician and Sportsmedicine,* August 1982, pp. 142–46.

Schwane, James A., and R. B. Armstrong. "Effect of Training on Skeletal Muscle Injury from Downhill Running in Rats." *Medicine and Science in Sports and Exercise,* vol. 15, no. 2, 1983, p. 165.

Schwane, James A., Scarlet R. Johnson, C. B. Vandenakker, and R. B. Armstrong. "Blood Markers of Delayed-Onset Muscular Soreness with Downhill Treadmill Running." *Medicine and Science in Sports and Exercise,* vol. 13, no. 2, 1981, p. 80.

Schwane, James A., Bruce G. Watrous, Scarlet R. Johnson, and R. B. Armstrong. "Is Lactic Acid Related to Delayed-Onset Muscle Soreness?" *The Physician and Sportsmedicine,* March 1983, pp. 124–31.

Siegel, A. J., M. J. Warhol, W. J. Evans, and L. M. Silverman. "Focal Myofibrillar Necrosis in Skeletal Muscle of Trained Marathon Runners after Competition." *Medicine and Science in Sports and Exercise,* vol. 15, no. 2, 1983, p. 164.

Smodlaka, Vojin. "Medical Aspects of Heading the Ball in Soccer." *The Physician and Sportsmedicine,* February 1984, pp. 127–31.

Stanish, William D. "Overuse Injuries in Athletes: A Perspective." *Medicine and Science in Sports and Exercise,* vol. 16, no. 1, 1984, pp. 1–7.

Wells, Thomas D., George T. Jessup, and Kathy S. Langlotz. "Effects of Sunscreen Use during Exercise in the Heat." *The Physician and Sportsmedicine,* June 1984, pp. 132–44.

Weltman, Arthur, and Bryant Stamford. "Beware When Exercising in the Heat." *The Physician and Sportsmedicine,* May 1983, p. 171.

Chapter 8

Especially for Women

Be a Sport

My good friend David is genial and good-natured. He does not strive to project a macho male image. He prefers white wine to beer, and I believe he eats quiche. Dave's sport is tennis, and once in a while when he notices a little bulge around his middle he will jog a couple of miles.

Dave knows I walk as a regular exercise. He respects my endurance and speed in the sport but will not take up walking as an exercise himself. Dave has no macho hangups, but he is still afraid he will look too silly.

There is a broad range of opinion on brisk walking and race-walking, some of it highly vocal. Starting with the positive—runners have the highest regard for walkers. They know that the speed that a race-walker can generate without losing touch with the ground is often faster than some of their fellow runners can maintain. They know that the Olympic 50-kilometer walk is farther than the Olympic marathon. Among runners, a race-walker can feel elitist.

Unfortunately, there is also negative opinion. It may be as mild as, "Maybe brisk walking is O.K. for women over 70 and post-coronary men, but I need real exercise."

More extreme negative opinion may be heard from the redneck sidelines. The comments are at best derogatory and sometimes bad enough to be unprintable. John Allen, a former Olympic race-walker, recently decided to try for a comeback. He worked out on the roads around his home town and was gaining good speed and stamina. He endured the occasional snide comment from a passing car, but when a pickup truck tried to sideswipe him, he really got mad. John called the police and wrote to the media about the incident, and I think he has been able to work out peaceably since then.

See the chapter on "Safekeeping" so you will be ready with a few sharp rejoinders for the vocal know-nothings.

There is a bright side. Because walking is commonly seen as not demanding in strength, speed, and mental toughness it is not intimidating to the novice. Walking as an exercise has a benign halo and is tried even by those who have never done anything more athletic than wrestling with a Black Russian at a cocktail party. Walking does not scare off even timid souls who otherwise are afraid of running, who never learned to ride a bike, or who are afraid to put their face in the water when swimming.

That brings us to some of the differences between men and women. The surveys and statistics say that women do not participate in sports as much as men do; also they are less successful than men in athletic competition. Many women simply don't consider themselves athletic.

Is this due to male-female differences in body structure and body chemistry? Or are there cultural reasons behind women's own poor self-image as athletes? Whatever the answer, even women who think of themselves as utterly uncoordinated have taken up walking. Fifty million people in the United States walk as a physical activity because walking acts as a tonic for them; and most of these walkers are women. Perhaps they walk because it is an easy exercise for a nonathlete, an exercise that doesn't involve throwing, catching, hitting, or running. No matter what the reason, they are out there putting one foot in front of the other, mile after mile.

A number of women have been courageous enough to try race-walking. The total number of participants in this sport is only in the thousands, but more than 60 percent of them are women, and that percentage is increasing as race-walking becomes more popular. Women do not enter the sport just for exercise; they are also fierce competitors.

In all walking races the women and men race on the same course at the same time, and the women do very well. In fact, in the Coney Island race, the oldest footrace in the nation, most of the recent winners have been women.

If the ratio of women to men becomes more disproportionate, I'm going to sound an alarm. We men must not abdicate our role in such a good sport as race-walking to women. I will exhort my brothers to bring in more males before the women tell us, "Sorry fellas, this is a woman's sport."

The Last Male Bastions

Though many women may have taken up walking because they

were brought up to be "feminine" (genteel, frail, and unathletic), some have never accepted that role. In almost every sport women have defied tradition by competing successfully in events once viewed as too dangerous or too challenging.

Women's ice hockey teams compete on collegiate levels. Women's basketball adopted men's rules and went professional. A few women professional boxers compete among themselves. Individual junior high school girls have made the boys' teams in soccer and football. Professional women jockeys ride their share of winners.

Several years ago, I was in a Masters track meet and found myself competing against a woman in the pole vault. I couldn't help thinking, "Well, the last male bastion in sports has finally fallen."

I spoke to my competitor during the meet and learned that she was actually the second woman pole vaulter. The first was a gymnast in California who reportedly vaulted over 9 feet.

When you think about it, there is good enough reason why a woman should pole vault well. The event does require upper body strength, but as important are speed down the runway and coordination in flying up and over the bar. Women sprinters have more than enough speed. Women gymnasts have not only the coordination but also plenty of strength in their arms and shoulders as shown by those incredible flying stunts on the uneven parallel bars. Pole vaulting? Of course!

Two other sports—lacrosse and rugby—have traditionally had an aura of old boy clubbiness about them. These are no longer male sports havens. Women are playing and have formed teams and leagues.

When the Australian national women's lacrosse team toured the United States in 1977, the players had a running program six days a week and circuit training with weights and resistance machines five days a week. An equal amount of time was spent sharpening timing, accuracy, and coordination with specific lacrosse drills. On top of that there were the intrasquad games.

Women's rugby teams play by the same international rules as men. Rugby is a game that you must see before you can appreciate its rigors. Watching from the sidelines it might seem like total anarchy, but there are a few rules. Blocking is not allowed, nor is "dangerous" tackling. Outside of that there is plenty of brute force in the scrums and much rough and tumble action in going after the ball whether loose or being carried. The game stops only once for 5 minutes at half time. Otherwise each half is 40 minutes of continuous play with no substitutions. Even when a player is tackled and is obliged by the rules to drop the ball, play continues. Everyone else goes after the loose ball, and no one stops to look after the guy who was tackled.

Like the men, most women players do not use the permitted kneepads and shin guards. Rugby's no game for the delicate or faint of heart.

Body building was once thought to be impenetrably male, and now there are major competitions for the women who pump iron. There is even a movie about them.

Last spring, I saw undeniable proof of female strength, endurance, and fearlessness. I spent a week aboard a 100-foot schooner that plied the waters around the Virgin Islands. The three members of the deck crew—Sophie, Allison, and Lisa—were responsible not just for swabbing the deck but for all types of work—such as raising the anchor and climbing 50 feet above the deck to work with the sails—that required brute power and nerve.

Anatomy and Destiny

It is clear that women can become strong, fast, well-coordinated, and fearless. It requires work and perseverence, just as with men. Of course, there are differences in anatomy and differences in hormone levels, but women can improve in all the ways that men can. The research has shown that, except for the reproductive systems, male-female differences are small.

Strength

The most significant difference between the sexes is in upper body strength. Men have stronger arms and shoulders in terms of both absolute strength and strength relative to lean body weight.

Jack H. Wilmore of the Exercise and Sport Science Laboratory of the University of Arizona recorded strength changes in men and women after a 10-week weight lifting program. The women gained significant strength in all muscle groups, including the upper body groups. The men were still stronger on an absolute scale, but the women had outpaced the men percentage-wise in the bench press, leg press, and grip strength.

Wilmore further compared the sexes in lower body strength and found the women to be weaker by 27 percent. When he measured lower body strength relative to lean body weight, however, the women were 5 percent *stronger* than the men.

Speed

Running performance in men and women was tested and analyzed by Philip B. Sparling and Kirk J. Cureton of the Human Performance Laboratory of the University of Georgia. The investigators measured, in male and female subjects, (1) aerobic power, (2) percentage of body fat, (3) running efficiency, and (4) how far they could run in 12 minutes.

The men ran farther than the women in the allotted time, were more efficient runners (i.e., used relatively less energy for an equal distance covered), were not as fat, and averaged higher in aerobic power (cardiorespiratory capacity).

Sparling and Cureton did some statistical analysis to see whether the differences in 12-minute run performances were related in any way to male-female sexual differences. They found that sex per se had a negligible influence on performance. Rather, 12-minute run performances were the result of oxygen power, body fat percentage, and running economy.

These conclusions were confirmed by R. R. Pate and the team of researchers at the Human Performance Laboratory of the University of South Carolina who studied men and women who had equal performance records in road-racing. When these subjects were tested for the same factors of oxygen capacity, body composition (percentage fat), and running economy, there were no statistical differences between the sexes.

Temperature

On the average, women do not tolerate hot weather as well as men do. Add work to the picture and heat will take an even greater toll on the women. A number of studies have shown that women's core temperatures rise higher than men's during heat exposure and especially during work in a hot environment. One of the body's mechanisms for reducing heat is sweating, but women don't sweat as much as men.

Enter: exercise. When endurance-trained women were placed at rest in a hot environment, their body temperatures remained at lower levels than the temperatures of nonathletic women and nonathletic men. One of the physiological mechanisms was increased, sweating. This study done by Yoshio Kobayashi and the researchers at the Human Performance Laboratory of Chukyo University and the Nagoya City University Medical School in Japan is considered applicable to all races.

Exercise Diets

It is generally conceded that men and women ordinarily process the food they eat in slightly different ways. Maybe so, but women athletes are not ordinary women. B. J. Konopka and E. M. Haymes at the Exercise Physiology Laboratory of Florida State University compared men and women athletes on high carbohydrate diets and very low carbohydrate diets. They found that both the women and men used a greater percentage of protein as an energy source when the diet was carbohydrate depleted. Athletes are athletes.

Tough Eggs

Serious male athletes have always considered themselves mentally hard as nails. Several past psychological studies of male runners showed so consistent a trend that a standard profile was developed using elite distance runners (see accompanying table).

Kay Porter, Ph.D., a sports psychologist in Eugene, Oregon, evaluated 20 female runners and found they had POMS (Profile of Mood States) scores that were remarkably similar to the standard profile for male runners, elite male runners at that. Tough eggs are tough eggs.

Profile of Mood States

(male elite distance runners)

Tension/Nervousness	decreased (−)
Depression/Dejection	decreased (− −)
Anger/Hostility	decreased (−)
Vigor/Activity	increased (+ + +)
Fatigue/Inertia	decreased (−)
Confusion/Bewilderment	decreased (− −)

Keeping Calcium

Women past menopause lose the benefits of high estrogen levels. One of the results is osteoporosis—the loss of calcium from the bones. But estrogen is not in complete charge of the mineralization or demineralization of bones. Dietary calcium plays a role; so does vitamin D; and so does exercise.

Nancy Oyster and her colleagues at Colorado State University found that among menopausal women the physically active had better calcified bones than the inactive. To isolate the effect of physical activity, subjects on hormone therapy were omitted from the study as were those with diets unusually rich in calcium and vitamin D.

Several other studies of menopausal women compared sedentary women with those in exercise programs. The athletes had significantly stronger bones.

In a longitudinal study Everett L. Smith, Ph.D., and others at the Biogerontology Laboratory at the Department of Preventive Medicine of the University of Wisconsin found that menopausal women had increased the mineral content of their bones following a mild but long-term exercise program.

If you are a woman past menopause, you can kick osteoporosis out of your life with exercise walking.

Too Soon Old?

Perhaps we become too soon old; but it's never too late to become smart. Women of any age can exercise and gain significant benefits.

The usually proffered excuse is, "I'm too old to start being an athlete." That does not mean that your body is too old, only that your self-image is old.

At the University of Western Ontario, D. Barr and J. S. Skinner trained two groups of women, one in their third decade (average age 23 years) and one in their fifth decade (average age 43.6 years). The women were trained at 70 percent of their maximum aerobic power for a period of eight weeks. The investigators found that the older women matched the younger women in rate of improvement in both oxygen capacity and power output.

At the Institute of Environmental Stress of the University of California, Barbara Drinkwater and her research team compared young women to much older women in resistance to heat stress and in functional sweating capacity. She found that the level of aerobic power was the only significant factor. If the level was high, women of every age tolerated heat stress better than women of low cardiovascular fitness.

Kay Porter's study of the psychological profiles of women runners, cited previously, included a group of women aged 35 to 63. Their Profiles of Mood States were very close to those of young women runners and—another surprise—young men runners.

Harri Suominen, Ph.Lic., and his fellow scientists at the Department of Public Health of the University of Jyraskyla, Finland, investigated the changes in muscle and connective tissue that occurred in a group of 69-year-old men and women after an eight-week exercise program in which walking-jogging was the principal activity. The men and women increased their aerobic power significantly and equally. The same was found to be true for connective tissue metabolism, a new area of investigation in the field of exercise physiology.

The final proof of the "never too old" theorem is Gwen C., who, at age 93, walks five days a week in Central Park. Gwen does not just stroll; she walks with determination, pumping her arms in race-walk style. More amazing still, she began to race-walk when she was in her late eighties. She started with short distances and modest speed and gradually became stronger. Now she does the full 6-mile loop of the park, come sun or rain or snow.

Let Gwen be your inspiration.

Advantage Women

As we have seen, women have to work hard at play just to stay even with men in several physical and physiologic areas. In upper body strength women cannot even match men in terms of absolute strength levels.

In some areas, though, it is advantage women.

Women have greater flexibility than men. Women also have more natural grace of movement. Add to these a greater hip width relative to height to help with a longer stride. Add further good lower body strength, and you have the qualities needed to excel in walking.

Flexibility and grace of movement are also two of the three qualities that give women exclusive rights to another aerobic exercise—belly dancing. Belly dancing is a true aerobic (metabolic) exercise as well as an art form.

In the late 1970s R. Gandee led a group of investigators from the University of Akron and Kent State University in a study of recreational belly dancing. They found that the average expenditure of energy was 372 calories per hour and concluded that belly dancing would be useful in exercise prescriptions for female patients.

Another advantage that women have over men is a natural means of heart protection. This is especially true of women athletes. Women have higher blood levels of high-density lipoproteins. HDL-C's, of all the blood lipids, are the only good guys. Their work is to help keep the coronary arteries clean.

In 1976 Yves Deshaies and Claude Allard of the Physical Sciences Laboratory of Laval University of Quebec had a splendid opportunity to study Olympic athletes during the Olympic Games in Montreal, and they were especially interested in lipid metabolism. They set up a mobile research laboratory in the Olympic Village and were able to work with 95 athletes from 22 nations.

One of their studies was the measurement of HDL-C levels in men and women in several sports. They found that the Olympic athletes' HDL-C levels were 20 percent above those cited for the general population of the same ages. The women Olympians had the highest HDL-C levels of all. As an example, male athletes in their upper twenties had an average HDL-C value of 57.3 (mg/dl), whereas female athletes of the same age reached 72.0 (mg/dl) levels.

Women Only

One physical achievement of women is denied to all men—child bearing. Most women who give birth to a child consider it the most momentous event of their lives. Great preparations are made— medical care for the mother and household readiness for the new child.

There are other preparations that go on in a woman's body even before she conceives, and these preparations are far more complex. They involve the brain, the pituitary gland, the ovaries, and the uterus. They involve four major hormones: follicle stimulating hormone and luteinizing hormone from the pituitary gland, and estrogen and progesterone from the ovaries. They involve constant change and interchange and a return to the starting point every month. And that is only the briefest outline.

The hormonal changes of the menstrual cycle are undaunted by the metabolic changes that take place with moderate exercise. On the other hand, exercise is independent of the different phases of the menstrual cycle.

Lou A. Stephenson and others at the Human Performance Laboratory of Indiana University recorded oxygen use at different exercise intensities at different times of the month in their female subjects. They found that the day of the cycle made no difference in oxygen utilization. They also measured carbon dioxide production, the ratio of carbohydrate:fat:protein used as fuel for exercise, and other metabolic functions at different exercise intensities at different times of the month for each subject. Again there were no differences from one time to another.

When exercise becomes heavy—long, hard, and frequent—all bets are off. Many women who perform serious physical activity have experienced a disruption in their cycles. Menstruation becomes irregular and less frequent; sometimes it stops completely.

The phenomenon has provided fertile ground for research, and there have been many studies. Some studies have been single-issue work. Some have examined more than one factor. Some have disagreed with others.

Here is a sampling of the evidence: among women athletes whose cycles have been disrupted, there are many:

- who run more than 40 miles per week;
- who are from different sports and physical disciplines, including distance running, rowing, swimming, basketball, and ballet;
- who do hard workouts;
- who have a low percentage of body fat, often below 15 percent;
- whose diet is low in protein;
- who are vegetarians;
- who show changes in some reproductive hormone levels (though the studies are inconsistent);
- whose body temperature is elevated during and after workouts.

With all the research that has been done—a review article in 1985 included a reference list of 86 papers, most of them directly concerned with amenorrhea—there has been no consensus as to the physiologic mechanisms involved. It seems likely from this observation post that several interrelated mechanisms are involved, and the effects are additive. If a threshold of hormonal change is reached, ovulation will be suppressed and endometrial change will not take place.

The athletes themselves do not seem greatly concerned by the dysfunction of their reproductive systems. If that is foolish, there seems to be Someone who looks after those who need to be cared for—athletic amenorrhea seems to be completely reversible when physical activity is diminished. The menstrual cycle is restored after a few months of rest or milder activity, and these women can usually become pregnant.

If extensive exercise causes such profound changes in monthly cyclical function, what about exercise during pregnancy?

There have been a few surveys, many personal reports, and as much folklore as you have patience to hear. A few experimental studies employing running or cycling have been done, but they have been limited for fear of causing harm to the fetus.

In Vermont, James F. Clapp III and Sherry Dickstein of the University of Vermont College of Medicine studied more than 300 pregnant women who, before conception, exercised regularly.

Vermont women seemed ripe for study. The authors state that 50 percent of women in the reproductive age range exercise frequently, half of them above an aerobic threshold.

In the study, running, cross-country skiing, and aerobic dance were the most popular exercises.

During pregnancy some women stopped exercising, some continued for up to 18 weeks, and some continued into their ninth month though usually at a reduced pace. Three research-tidy groups were thus formed.

The results showed that those who exercised throughout pregnancy:

- gained the least weight, averaging 12 pounds;

- delivered earlier, seven days before term on average;

- had babies with lower birth weight, usually about 1 pound less;

- did not have any more complications of labor and delivery than the other groups.

In a recent review of the investigations into exercise during pregnancy, Jan Gorski at the Department of Physiology of the Bialystok Medical School in Poland presented several findings of concern. Some of these findings fall into natural pairs:

- In pregnancy, blood volume increases and a relative anemia results.
- Exercise diverts a large percentage of total blood volume to the working muscles.

- Exercising aerobically can raise body temperature by 2 or 3 degrees and, in hot environments, even higher.
- Hyperthermia can adversely affect the fetus in the first trimester.

- During exercise, adrenaline and noradrenaline blood levels increase.
- These amines (adrenaline and noradrenaline) will increase blood pressure and affect uterine contractility.

- Fetal heart rate was not affected by walking or bicycling, but jogging increased fetal heart rate.
- In pregnancies with placental insufficiency, exercise increased fetal heart rate.

The author concludes that mild to moderate exercise during pregnancy is well-tolerated and causes no harm. But, he cautions, watch out anyway.

The American College of Obstetricians and Gynecologists, not a radical organization, recognized the sports and fitness revolution in 1985 by formulating guidelines for exercise during pregnancy. Amid a rash of precautionary information these specialists approve brisk walking, swimming, and stationary cycling. The College frowns on water skiing, surfing, and scuba diving.

Pregnancy is a special state of being, and the School of Good Sense says that moderation is the watchword for exercise. When in doubt, do less; and share the responsibility with your M.D.

Walking as an exercise seems to suit the world of equal rights. Women can participate, even compete, on an equal footing with men.

But I urge you women not to try to appropriate walking just for yourselves. Be gracious instead, and encourage more of us men to join you in a great sport. There's room for us both.

References

Barr, D., and J. S. Skinner. "Trainability of Women in Their Third and Fifth Decade." *Medicine and Science in Sports and Exercise,* vol. 13, no. 2, 1981, p. 93.

Bonen, Arend, and Hans K. Keizer. "Athletic Menstrual Cycle Irregularity: Endocrine Responses to Exercise and Training." *The Physician and Sportsmedicine,* August 1984, pp. 78–94.

Brooks, S. M., C. F. Sanborn, B. H. Albrecht, and W. W. Wagner, Jr. "Athletic Amenorrhea: The Role of Diet." *Medicine and Science in Sports and Exercise,* vol. 16, no. 2, 1984, p. 117.

Bullen, Beverly A., Gary S. Skrinar, Inese Z. Beitins, Gretchen vonMering, Barry A. Turnbull, and Janet W. McArthur. "Induction of Menstrual Disorders by Strenuous Exercise in Untrained Women." *The New England Journal of Medicine,* vol. 312, no. 21, 1985, pp. 1349–53.

Carlberg, Karen A., Marie T. Buckman, Glenn T. Peake, and Marvin L. Riedesel. "Body Composition of Oligo/Amenorrheic Athletes." *Medicine and Science in Sports and Exercise,* vol. 15, no. 3, 1983, pp. 215–17.

Clapp, James F., III, and Sherry Dickstein. "Endurance Exercise and Pregnancy Outcome." *Medicine and Science in Sports and Exercise,* vol. 16, no. 6, 1984, pp. 556–62.

Cowan, Mary M., and Larry W. Gregory. "Responses of Pre- and Post-Menopausal Females to Aerobic Conditioning." *Medicine and Science in Sports and Exercise,* vol. 17, no. 1, 1985, pp. 138–43.

Deshaies, Yves, and Claude Allard. "Serum High-Density Lipoprotein Cholesterol in Male and Female Olympic Athletes." *Medicine and Science in Sports and Exercise,* vol. 14, no. 3, 1982, pp. 207–11.

Drinkwater, Barbara L., J. F. Bedi, A. B. Loucks, S. Roche, and S. M. Horvath. "Sweating Sensitivity and Capacity of Adult and Post-Menopausal Women." *Medicine and Science in Sports and Exercise,* vol. 14, no. 2, 1982, p. 126.

Freedson, Patty S., Patricia Mihevic, Anne B. Loucks, and Robert N. Girandola. "Physique, Body Composition and Psychological Characteristics of Competitive Female Body Builders." *The Physician and Sportsmedicine,* May 1983, pp. 85–93.

Gandee, R., B. Hallering, A. Maluke, Jr., and J. Adolph. "The Energy Cost of Recreational Dancing." Abstracts of 25th Annual Meeting of American College of Sports Medicine, vol. 10, no. 1, 1978, p. 54.

Gorski, Jan. "Exercise during Pregnancy: Maternal and Fetal Responses. A Brief Review." *Medicine and Science in Sports and Exercise,* August 1985, pp. 407–16.

Haymes, E. M., G. D. Cartee, S. M. Rape, E. S. Garcia, and T. E. Temples. "Thermal and Metabolic Responses of Men and Women during Exercise in Cold and Neutral Environments." *Medicine and Science in Sports and Exercise,* vol. 14, no. 2, 1982, p. 126.

Kindig, Louise E., Patricia L. Soares, Joseph M. Wisenbaker, and Sam R. Mrvos. "Standard Scores for Women's Weight Training." *The Physician and Sportsmedicine,* October 1984, pp. 67–74.

Kobayashi, Yoshio, Yoshire Ando, Noriaki Okuda, Shozo Takaba, and Kokici Ohara. "Effects of Endurance Training on Thermoregulation in Females." *Medicine and Science in Sports and Exercise,* vol. 12, no. 5, 1980, pp. 361–64.

Loucks, A. B., and S. M. Horvath. "Endocrine Status of Amenorrheic and Eumenorrheic Runners." *Medicine and Science in Sports and Exercise,* April 1984, p. 118.

———. "The Participation of the Female Athlete in Long-Distance Running." (Opinion statement of the American College of Sports Medicine.) *Medicine and Science in Sports,* vol. 11, no. 4, 1979, pp. ix–xi.

Morrow, James, R., and W. W. Hosler. "Strength Comparisons in Untrained Men and Trained Women Athletes." *Medicine and Science in Sports and Exercise,* vol. 13, no. 3, 1981, pp. 194–97.

Oyster, Nancy, Max Morton, and Sheri Linnell. "Physical Activity and Osteoporosis in Post-Menopausal Women." *Medicine and Science in Sports and Exercise,* vol. 16, no. 1, 1984, pp. 44–50.

Pate, R. R., C. Barnes, and W. Miller. "A Physiological Comparison of Performance-Matched Male and Female Distance Runners." *Medicine and Science in Sports and Exercise,* vol. 14, no. 2, 1982, p. 139.

Porter, Kay. "Psychological Characteristics of the Average Female Runner." *The Physician and Sportsmedicine,* May 1985, pp. 171–75.

Sanborn, C. F., B. H. Albrecht, and W. W. Wagner, Jr. "Athletic Amenorrhea: The Role of Body Fat." *Medicine and Science in Sports and Exercise,* vol. 16, no. 2, 1984, p. 118.

Smith, Everett L., and Catherine Gilligan. "Physical Activity Prescription for the Older Adult." *The Physician and Sportsmedicine,* August 1983, pp. 91–101.

Stephenson, Lou A., Margaret Kolka, and James E. Wilkerson. "Metabolic and Thermoregulatory Responses to Exercise during the Human Menstrual Cycle." *Medicine and Science in Sports and Exercise,* vol. 14, no. 4, 1982, pp. 270–75.

Suominen, Harri, Eino Heikkinen, and Terttu Parkatti. "Effect of Eight Weeks' Physical Training on Muscle and Connective Tissue of the M. Vastus Lateralis in 69-Year-Old Men and Women." *Journal of Gerontology,* vol. 32, 1977, pp. 33–37.

Vander, Lauren B., Barry A. Franklin, David Wrisley, and Melvyn Rubenfire. "Cardiorespiratory Responses to Arm and Leg Ergometry in Women." *The Physician and Sportsmedicine,* May 1984, pp. 101–6.

Wakat, Diane K., Kathleen A. Sweeney, and Alan D. Rogol. "Reproductive System Function in Women Cross-Country Runners." *Medicine and Science in Sports and Exercise,* vol. 14, no. 4, 1982, pp. 263–69.

Wells, Christine L., and Sharon A. Plowman. "Sexual Difference in Athletic Performance: Biological or Behavioral?" *The Physician and Sportsmedicine,* August 1983, pp. 52–63.

Wilmore, Jack H. "Inferiority of the Female Athlete: Myth or Reality?" *Rx Sports and Travel,* March/April 1975, pp. 19–22.

Withers, R. T. "Physiological Responses of International Female Lacrosse Players to Pre-Season Conditioning." *Medicine and Science in Sports,* vol. 10, no. 4, 1978, pp. 238–42.

Chapter 9

The Age of Youth, the Youth of Age
Perpetual Fitness

I have five older friends who, as of this writing, range in age from their mid-seventies to their early eighties. They are scattered geographically and do not know each other, but they share the characteristic of mental vigor, even a little feistiness. They have taught me that I need not be old just by virtue of having spent many years on this earth. If I become old, it will be because I have not taken the opportunity to be young.

All five friends—Dave, Paul, Berenice, José, and Red—are leprechauns in spirit.

Dave is out in the early morning, four days a week, walking for fitness and self-challenge.

Paul experiments with new glazes from raw materials for his wheel-thrown pottery.

Berenice no longer makes photographs, but she keeps up with current political and economic affairs and sees events from a unique perspective. She was a struggling artist in Paris in the 1920s, saw the Great Depression on both sides of the Atlantic, and lived through World War II and the incredible technological revolution of the post-war era. Artistic recognition came late, after the age of 60.

José teaches poetry, writing with an uncanny eye and ear for form and rhythm, for language and essences. His angel/devil personality is ageless.

Red is as imaginative as ever in his woodworking and mechanical skills. When someone comes to him with a prized possession needing repair (anything from a broken toy to a staved-in fishing boat), Red will finish the job with a fine touch. He will then stand back and admire his own work with a smile.

All five are young at heart and have a glint in their eyes. Four of the five are a little frail physically or physiologically. Only Dave is as young *of* heart as he is young at heart. Dave is the walker.

Sports by the Year

There are a good number of older athletes whose sports include running, cycling, swimming, and rowing, as well as walking. They have escaped the rapid descent generally associated with aging. They show only small declines in protein synthesis, capacity for oxygen uptake, maximum heart rate, mineralization of bone, immune system strength, and resistance of the cardiovascular system to disease and injury. (That is only half the list.)

Decline does occur. Fifty-year-olds do not win Olympic gold medals. But the decline can be at less than half the expected rate.

These older athletes have sparked some interest from the exercise physiologists and a few of the cardiologists. There is a curiosity about a group of people related to each other only by their refusal to accept the common dictum that age brings ravages.

The investigators designed a scattering of experiments involving exercise training in older people. One study examined brain range; others looked at body works.

There were different parameters of heart rate to check: resting heart rate, maximal heart rate with exercise, and recovery heart rate after exercise.

The oxygen delivery system—lungs to heart to arteries to cells—needed to be compared in old and young and in trained and untrained individuals.

The calcification of bones was another area in which to gain knowledge.

Cellular aging might allow a few more of its secrets to be unlocked with the key of endurance exercise.

The investigations went forth, but there were few replicative studies and little coordination of efforts. Reports appeared in the sports medicine literature from time to time, but they were not greeted with full orchestral fanfare.

Gradually, over the years, a body of knowledge has come into being, and the results are enlightening. Here are the findings of some of the studies:

- Two groups of men, one aged 65 years (average) and the other 26 years (average) showed close to the same percentage increase in cardiovascular reserve with bicycle ergometer training. In both, there were large increases in anaerobic threshold and in cardiovascular function under submaximal work loads.

- Two groups of women marathoners, one aged 25 (average) and the other 38 (average), were compared. All facets of cardiovascular function were close to equal in both groups except for resting heart rate. The young group had an average heart rate of 44 per minute and the older group's average heart rate was 56 per minute, a significant difference but both sharply lower than the sedentary controls who had an average rate of 76 per minute.

- A group of 50-year-old women who exercised 45 minutes a day, three days a week, was observed over a period of three and a half years. In a control group, bone mineral content declined 2.4 percent per year. In the exercise group bone mineral content declined the first year and then *increased* for the next two and a half years!

- Cognitive function (thought processing) was measured in a cross-sectional study of runners and sedentary people in four age groups, from third decade (20–29 years) to sixth decade (50–59 years). In the sedentary control groups the speed of decision and discrimination process was progressively slower with increasing age. In the runners there were no significant differences in cognitive function between age groups. The 50- to 59-year-old runners were as quick as the 20- to 29-year-olds!

Stepping back a pace from the details of the aging process, a broader concept comes into focus. It is a question of chickens and eggs. In the declines in function, vigor, and physical performance seen with advancing years, is the primary process one of aging? The answer now seems to be that half the process is one of aging, and the other half is a deficiency disease—an inadequate amount of physical activity. In other words, the decline in vigor and physical performance is caused, 50 percent, by the decrease in the vigor of physical performance. Age is as much the result of the signs of aging as it is the cause.

The older athletes provide evidence from one direction that exercise lack is a deficiency disease. There is also evidence from the opposite direction. In younger people, in their twenties and thirties, an enforced sedentary lifestyle will bring about declines in: muscle mass, protein balance, oxygen utilization capacity, cardiovascular vigor, structural strength of bones . . . all the same decrements seen in aging and all caused entirely by a deficiency of activity.

We cannot stay young as the birthdays go by, but we can be youthful. Spirit and outlook are not a matter of age. Our bodies, too, need not be so old. Being physically active is the way, and the best choice of all is walking.

The Skin Game

"O.K.," you say. "So exercise will help my heart and strengthen my aging bones, but what do I do about these wrinkles? When I look in the mirror I don't see cardiovascular reserve and maximal oxygen uptake; I see wrinkles."

There have been no cross-sectional or longitudinal studies of wrinkling in active versus lazy people. There is only the common observation that old people have wrinkles and young people do not. Until the studies are done I can only offer you one personal observation.

For several years I had baggy tissues under my eyes. It is a family trait, and I had always accepted the skin that covered my bones. In my early forties the condition (notice, it became a condition) worsened, and I even gave some thought to plastic surgery.

It was about the time that I started to use walking as metabolic exercise.

Somehow, eight years went by and because of various time-consuming activities I never did get over to the plastic surgeon. One day my wife looked at me in a puzzled way and said, "You know, you don't have bags under your eyes anymore."

I looked in the mirror, and sure enough, they were mostly gone. The change had been so gradual that neither I nor anyone else had noticed until then.

I thought about any life changes that could have brought about the miracle. The only large positive change was my exercise walking regimen.

Can endurance walking give you a nonsurgical facelift? Perhaps. Exercise does change calcium, potassium, carbohydrate, fat, and protein metabolism. Why not the elements that go into connective tissues, too? In fact, there is evidence that active older people do have firmer skin than others of their age group. It's worth a chance. Be your own doctor—no scalpels, injections, pills, or fad diets. It's a risk-free opportunity, and you won't even get a medical bill.

Second Adolescence

It is all to the good, and admirable, for athletes to continue their exercise regimen beyond the age at which they can compete with the 20-year-olds. But what of those who have left the playing fields for the work of society—the professions and industry, the "real world"? They may not be doing much more than exercising options or passing the buck. Can they achieve the youth of their still-active age-mates? And what of those who never knew vigorous play, even in their youth?

The answer is a clamorous, "Yes, you can start at point zero on the fitness scale and finish with the finely tuned machine that your body can be." It will take effort and it will take time; but the potential for fitness remains in your tissues through your sixties and probably until 75.

Two Canadian studies looked into the effect of exercise on the aerobic power of older subjects. The University of Toronto study showed that older subjects who had been physically inactive for many years achieved a 29 percent gain in aerobic power with an exercise program of proper frequency, distance, and intensity. The University of Western Ontario study compared women in their twenties (23 years average) and their forties (44 years average). The investigators concluded that with comparable training schedules the improvement in aerobic power was the same for both age groups.

Whatever your age, whatever your previous activity, whatever the pace you are able to keep—walking will point you in the right direction. Just follow your feet, and the fountain of youth will appear.

Paint the Revolution a Variegated Gray

The fitness revolution may have started with the young, but a good number of not-so-young refused to be left behind to molder. They took up running, walking, cycling, swimming, rowing, tennis, and skiing, just to name a few of the sports. They called themselves

Masters, Seniors, or Veterans to take on the mantle of experience in their chosen sports. Many grouped together to form clubs and associations. The Masters Sports Association, the Alden Ocean Shell Association, the U.S. Cycling Federation, the 70-Plus Ski Club, and Super Senior Tennis are just a few of the many.

The numbers of over–40-year-old athletes increased, and after a while the national temples of sports—A.A.U., T.A.C., U.S.T.A., etc.—welcomed the older athletes. Now, Masters athletes from almost every sport can find camaraderie and competition among their peers.

A few states responded positively by organizing state games to include all ages. Pennsylvania became a pioneer by holding Senior Games.

The revolution turned establishment, and now no end is in sight. The President's Council on Physical Fitness sets population goals by age group for participation in physical activity. For the over-65 age population, the Council wants to see over half of all the people involved. For senior citizens, the Council suggests less strenuous activities, and walking leads the list. How refreshing to see wisdom in high places.

Decades

"Become an athlete at my age?" you ask.

I need not even ask your age. The answer is, "It is easier now than when you were in your teens."

Now you do not have the self-doubt of the young. Now there is an assuredness born of the experience of years. You can select a sport for yourself; you can decide on the intensity at which to train; you can go for high performance or not, as you wish. You can make judgments based on knowing your own body, without the need for a coach's say so.

Each decade there is a new advantage gained—patience, tenacity, toughness. I am now in my early fifties and know many members of the race-walking community in the Northeast. In the fifties age group, there are some super competitors. Often, someone in his fifties will have a better performance time than all of the 40-year-olds. Often, two or three of the 50-year-olds will take the measure of all but the very best of the forties.

The spirit and vigor of the 50-year-olds was brought sharply into focus one day last year. I was doing a workout with Bob and

Mike, two walking friends with whom I occasionally share a lane in Prospect Park. Mike seemed to be pressing a faster-than-usual pace.

I said, "Mike, the race isn't until next week."

He said, "That's exactly it. My fiftieth birthday is in ten days and next week's race is the last chance I get to win a trophy. After that I'll be up against all you tigers."

Maybe a year at fifty will toughen Mike a bit. I am a couple of years up on Mike and have found, with toughness, an ability to not be tough. I have learned to be relaxed now that vigor has become integral to my being.

Each decade will bring surprises and clarifications. Keep your eyes open wide.

Sampling Centuries

Many efforts have been made to increase human life span. Experiments with caloric restriction, dietary antioxidants, immune cell transplants, and enzymes and hormone administration have all resulted in increases in the normal life span of laboratory animals. The research is important to our understanding of the aging process at the molecular, cellular, and total organism levels, but from a practical outlook, we also ought to examine the human life span as it stands right now.

Maximum life span for *Homo sapiens* has been variously estimated at 120 to 140 years, and I don't know anyone in town who has made it that far.

There are a few isolated cultures where people are reported to live out their life span years. What is more extraordinary is that they maintain their vitality—their mental sharpness and physical vigor—throughout their years.

The three cultures that have been studied the most are the Hunzas of Pakistan, the Abkhasians of the Soviet Union, and the Vilacabambans of Ecuador. Every detail of their lives has been examined with an eye to finding the secret of their longevity.

None of the researchers came up with anything strong enough to base a unified field theory on. None, that is, except the Russian physician Georgi Z. Pitskhelauri, M.D., who studied the Abkhasians and concluded, "Laziness, idleness, and parasitism are the enemies of health and longevity."

The factors that influence aging are like highway traffic signs:

- Slow, Pedestrian Crossing
- Exit for Roadside Stand. Fresh Fruit and Vegetables Daily
- Slow, People Working
- Rest Area Ahead
- Slow, Dear Crossings

In these long-lived cultures, walking is the most consistent common factor. The Abkhasians make walking a natural part of their lives. A typical day can be outlined as follows: awaken; personal hygiene; *stroll;* breakfast; *walk to work;* work; lunch; nap; work; *walk home;* dinner; leisure (music, visiting, etc.); *evening stroll;* bed. The Vilacabambans walk to the fields for their food, to the shrine in the mountains, and to the forest to gather wood. They also tread liquid clay to make into adobe brick. The Hunzas walk to work at tea plantations, orchards, and farms where the work itself involves much walking. Some of the centenarians walk to other villages several miles distant two or three times a week.

We, too, can take walking into our lives. We cannot all live in glacial valleys, or even in isolated communities. Some of us don't have time for afternoon naps. But almost everyone can walk. Most of us do walk in our daily activities and sometimes just for pleasure. Why not make your walking metabolic? Perhaps it can add years to your life. Certainly it can add life to your years.

References

Barr, D., and J. S. Skinner. "Trainability of Women in Their Third and Fifth Decade." *Medicine and Science in Sports and Exercise,* vol. 13, no. 2, 1981, p. 93.

Bruce, Robert A. "Exercise, Functional Aerobic Capacity, and Aging— Another Viewpoint." *Medicine and Science in Sports and Exercise,* vol. 16, no. 1, 1984, pp. 8–13.

Cowan, Mary M., and Larry W. Gregory. "Responses of Pre- and Post-Menopausal Females to Aerobic Conditioning." *Medicine and Science in Sports and Exercise,* vol. 17, no. 1, 1985, pp. 138–43.

Cunningham, L. N., C. Labrie, J. S. Soeldner, R. E. Gleason, and N. Anderson. "Aging and Running Related to Peripheral Blood Flow." *Medicine and Science in Sports and Exercise,* vol. 14, no. 2, 1982, p. 165.

Davies, K. J. A., L. Packer, and G. A. Brooks. "Mitochondrial Biogenesis and Exercise Energetics." *Medicine and Science in Sports and Exercise,* vol. 13, no. 2, 1981, p. 118.

Davis, J. A., M. H. Frank, B. J. Whipp, and K. Wasserman. "Anaerobic Threshold Alterations Consequent to Endurance Training in Middle-Aged Men." *Medicine and Science in Sports,* vol. 11, no. 1, 1979, p. 96.

DeVries, H. A., R. A. Wiswell, G. Romero, T. Moritani, and R. Bulbulian. "Comparison of Oxygen Kinetics in Old and Young Well-Conditioned Men." *Medicine and Science in Sports,* vol. 11, no. 1, 1979, p. 96.

Drinkwater, Barbara L., J. F. Bedi, A. B. Loucks, S. Roche, and S. M. Horvath. "Sweating Sensitivity and Capacity of Adult and Post-Menopausal Women." *Medicine and Science in Sports and Exercise,* vol. 14, no. 2, 1982, p. 126.

Faulkner, John A. "Skeletal Muscle De-Conditioning, Aging and Disease." (Delivered before the American Academy of Physical Medicine and Rehabilitation, Session 4, October 1980).

Hartung, G. H., R. S. Reeves, A. Sigurdson, D. Pullin, J. P. Foreyt, and W. Blocker. "Effects of a Low-Fat Diet on Plasma Lipids, Lipoproteins, and Cardiac Arrhythmias in Middle-Aged Runners." *Medicine and Science in Sports and Exercise,* vol. 15, no. 2, 1983, pp. 90–91.

Higuchi, M., L.-J. Cartier, and John O. Holloszy. "The Effects of Endurance Training on Free Radical Scavenging Enzymes in Rats." *Medicine and Science in Sports and Exercise,* vol. 15, no. 2, 1983, p. 93.

Kiessling, K.-H., L. Pilström, J. Karlsson, and Karen Piehl. "Mitochondrial Volume in Skeletal Muscle from Young and Old Physically Untrained and Trained Healthy Men and from Alcoholics." *Clinical Science,* 1973, pp. 547–54.

Pitskhelauri, Georgi Z. *The Longliving of Soviet Georgia.* New York: Human Sciences Press, 1982.

Sager, Kayleen. "Exercises to Activate Seniors." *The Physician and Sportsmedicine,* May 1984, pp. 144–51.

———. "Senior Fitness—for the Health of It." *The Physician and Sportsmedicine,* October 1983, pp. 31–36.

Schneider, Edward L., and John D. Reed, Jr. "Life Extension." *The New England Journal of Medicine,* vol. 312, no. 18, 1985, pp. 1159–68.

Sheehan, George. "Peaking for Life." *The Physician and Sportsmedicine,* July 1982, p. 32.

Sidney, K. H., and Roy J. Shephard. "Frequency and Intensity of Exercise Training for Elderly Subjects." *Medicine and Science in Sports,* vol. 10, no. 2, 1978, pp. 125–32.

Smith, Everett L., and Catherine Gilligan. "Physical Activity Prescription for the Older Adult." *The Physician and Sportsmedicine,* August 1983, pp. 91–101.

Smith, Everett L., P. E. Smith, C. P. Ensing, and M. M. Shea, "Exercise in Middle-Aged Women Decreases Bone Involution." *Medicine and Science in Sports and Exercise,* vol. 16, no. 2, 1984, p. 104.

Stamford, Bryant. "Exercise and Longevity." *The Physician and Sportsmedicine,* June 1984, p. 209.

Strovas, Jane. "Seniors Walk Away from Sedentary Life." *The Physician and Sportsmedicine,* April 1984, pp. 144–52.

Suominen, Harri, Eino Heikkinen, and Terttu Parkatti. "Effect of Eight Weeks' Physical Training on Muscle and Connective Tissue of the M. Vastus Lateralis in 69-Year-Old Men and Women." *Journal of Gerontology,* vol. 32, 1977, p. 33–37.

Upton, S. Jill, R. Donald Hagan, Barbara Lease, Joel Rosentswieg, Larry R. Gettman, and John J. Duncan. "Comparative Physiologic Profiles among Young and Middle-Aged Female Distance Runners." *Medicine and Science in Sports and Exercise,* vol. 16, no. 1, 1984, pp. 67–71.

Vailas, A. C., V. A. Pedrini, A. Pedrini-Mille, and John O. Holloszy. "Aging and Exercise: Ligament and Tendon Ground Substance." *Medicine and Science in Sports and Exercise,* vol. 14, no. 2, 1982, p. 106.

Weber, F., R. J. Barnard, and D. Roy. "Effects of an Intensive Short-Term Nutrition and Exercise Program on Individuals Age 70 and Older." *Medicine and Science in Sports and Exercise,* vol. 14, no. 2, 1982, p. 179.

Chapter 10

In Good Company
Pedestrians from Many Walks of Life

Although the ancients from Babylon to Thebes to Memphis to Troy generally walked to get from place to place, they took it as a chore, not a pleasure. Where possible they found other ways to get around.

The Phoenicians preferred sailing, and they roamed the entire Mediterranean Sea, even venturing out past Gibraltar into the Atlantic Ocean. The Carthaginians liked walking in North Africa no better than they liked it back home on the coast of Asia Minor. The most suitable alternative, they found, was the horse. The horse was not the only alternative for the anti-walking brigades. In 219 B.C. Hannibal and his senior officers rode astride elephants as they drove north in Spain to capture Seguntum, setting off the Second Punic War.

Diogenes: There were a few wise men of the time who did not begrudge having been born too soon to have a Lamborghini to tool around in. Diogenes was a shining example of living simply, walking everywhere, and using his physical abilities as nature had provided.

He studied philosophy with Antisthenes, the founder of the Cynic School of philosophy. The teacher walked daily from Piraeus, where he lived, to Athens, more than 4 miles away.

Diogenes went several steps beyond his teacher, traveling widely as a citizen of the world, a *kosmopolites*. As an aesthete with no possessions other than a clever tongue he became widely known throughout the Hellenic world. Some say his fame was second only to Alexander (III) the Great, his contemporary.

Aristotle: Aristotle studied many years with Plato at the Academy—too many, some say—and only on the death of the master philosopher did Aristotle take to wandering. He spent some years walking the countryside of the island of Lesbos, studying its natural history.

131

In 334 B.C. Aristotle returned to Athens to start a school of philosophy and rhetoric, but walking was still in his blood. At the Lyceum, Aristotle discoursed as he walked around the gardens, the covered walks, and the nearby countryside. His students followed him in his outdoor wandering classroom and were called peripatetics. The word originally referred to the covered walks (*peripatoi*) of the Lyceum but has come into our language to mean walking about. In walking, Aristotle no doubt considered himself the servant of Apollo Luceus, god of shepherds, to whom the grounds and buildings of his Lyceum were dedicated.

The Poets and Writers

Walking provides an environment that encourages stream-of-consciousness thinking. Subconscious processes are eased into action as well. It is in such a seeming anarchy of thought that metaphors are found. Poets over the ages have known or felt this connection between walking and poetry, for many of them were avid walkers.

The English School

The British Romantic poets of the early nineteenth century—Wordsworth, Coleridge, Shelley, and Keats among them—were persistent pedestrians who made walking a natural part of their lives. Most of them wrote about the beauty of nature and had little choice but to do their observations on foot. That was the first step of the creative process. Second, they had to tie their observations to their imagination, and here walking was the catalyst.

William Wordsworth, in 1790 at age 20, sailed to the European continent for a grand tour of France, Switzerland, and Italy. He walked 350 miles in the first two weeks and then continued his explorations at a more leisurely pace through the three countries, including the Alps, all on foot.

For many years thereafter, Wordsworth walked his beloved Lake Region gathering inspiration for his poems. Some of his contemporaries judged his total walking there to be over 100,000 miles. There is a tale that when a traveler wishing to see Wordsworth asked to be shown to his study, Wordsworth's housekeeper replied that his library was at the house but his study was out of doors.

Samuel Taylor Coleridge was also an inveterate walker, averaging 10 miles a day. It was on a walking tour with Wordsworth that he worked out the framework for *The Rime of the Ancient Mariner*. Coleridge was considered one of the great minds of the age by his contemporaries who often formed this opinion upon walking with the poet and listening to his discourse.

One Sunday John Keats, 23 years younger than Coleridge, saw the older poet talking to a colleague from Guy's Hospital and joined them. The three began to walk and for nearly 2 miles Coleridge held forth in conversation. Keats was astounded by the breadth and depth of Coleridge's knowledge and by the eloquence of his phrasing. In a letter to his brother George, Keats described the meeting and listed the variety of subjects discussed. Included were: nightingales, metaphysics, dreams, levels of consciousness, will versus volition, monsters, and the telling of a ghost story.

Keats, though frail, was a walker in his own right. In the spring of 1818 he walked north through England, 20 miles or more per day through the Lake Region and North Country, to reach Scotland. There he became more sharply convinced that human nature was to be his primary concern and nature secondary.

Percy Bysshe Shelley, about the same age as Keats, was also a confirmed walker. While at Oxford as a student, he would often walk to London, 40 miles distant. When he and Mary Wollstonecraft decided to elope they crossed the Channel and, once in France, set out on foot for Switzerland. In the first week they walked 100 miles and probably would have made it to that country had Shelley not turned his ankle in a hole in the road.

Walking, always a British tradition, was an avocation of other literary figures—James Boswell and Dr. Samuel Johnson, who toured the Hebrides together; Jane Austen, who made walkers of her heroines; and Thomas Carlyle, Lord Byron, Sir Walter Scott, and Charles Dickens, just to name a few.

The Americans

From the pioneer days to the present, Americans have been hikers. They have gone out to cross rugged terrain, always prepared for adversity. The American literary figures of the mid-nineteenth century, however, were more walkers in the tradition of the British writers.

Henry David Thoreau was one of the best. He was a phenomenal traveler who would walk 10 or 20 miles just to see a new landscape, even a single farmhouse he had not seen before.

Thoreau felt the need for a long walk in the woods, through fields and over hills each day just to preserve his health and spirit. Partly it was the walking and partly being "free from all worldly engagements."

He separated his walking from "taking exercise . . . as the swinging of dumbbells." Walking was, instead, an adventure of each day.

Walking for Thoreau became a matter of philosophy. Walkers, he said, were in a class by themselves, a "fourth estate outside of Church, State, and People."

And that from a writer.

Thoreau, when he was just 20 years old, walked with Ralph Waldo Emerson and brought new insights to the older poet/essayist. Emerson and Thoreau walked to the cliff, and at night Emerson looked up to see "a glimmering star and heard a frog." He asked himself, "Well, do not these suffice? Ponder it Emerson."

Emerson knew that walking is an art that is developed only by those who persist, and he believed that few know how to walk properly. He listed as requisites "endurance, plain clothes, old shoes, an eye for nature, good humor . . . good silence." He thought there was a need for a book that might be called *The Art of Walking,* but he never did write it.

It took Walt Whitman, breaker of the icons of poetry, to directly celebrate walking and wanderlust. In "Song of the Open Road" from his *Leaves of Grass* (Boston: Thayer and Eldridge, 1860–1861), the open road is a metaphorical pathway as well; but Whitman, a walker himself, also praises the act of walking.

Afoot and light-hearted I take to the open road.

. . . .

I inhale great draughts of space.

For the Record

In the nineteenth century another breed of walker appeared, more athletic than the poets. It was the record seeker. Sometimes the record seeker would attempt to break an existing record for speed or distance, and sometimes he would finesse the book by redefining the rules.

Records were sought in terms of distance, up to and including once around the world.

Records were sought in terms of the shortest time for a given distance. Los Angeles to New York was a popular distance course and the record is now just under 54 days.

Records were sought in terms of miles and consecutive hours. One thousand miles in 1,000 consecutive hours, 1 mile in each hour, was considered a noteworthy feat. That record fell early in the nineteenth century and the next goal was 1,000 miles in 1,000 consecutive half hours. Richard Manks made it in 1851.

Edward Payson Weston

Weston, an American, was the best known walker of the late 1800s. He had a free, flowing style of walking that was popularly called the "wobble."

As a young man, Weston was employed by the *Boston Herald* as a messenger and later as a reporter. He distinguished himself by his speed afoot and often scooped a story thereby.

He made his British walking debut in Scotland with an attempt at 55 miles in 12 hours. He wore a costume of boots, leggings, velvet pants, shirt, and linen hat. Toward the end of the 55 miles he had enough time to spare that he walked a half mile backwards and a half mile playing the cornet.

Back in the United States, a couple of years later, he walked from Boston to Washington, D.C., to see the inauguration of Abraham Lincoln.

Weston walked the width of the country several times. When he was 71 years old, he walked from ocean to ocean both ways, first from New York to San Francisco in 105 days and then from Los Angeles to New York in 76 days.

The fiercest competitive event of the time was the six-day race. (Never on Sunday.) Weston was good, usually walking well over 400 miles, but often the competition was better. The six-day record was broken repeatedly by other Americans and by Englishmen, though Weston once held the record briefly at 550 miles. In 1888, James Albert, an American, did an incredible 621 miles. The British thereupon sent George Littlewood—perhaps a Vulcan with a British accent—to complete over 623 miles in 140 hours (4 hours short of 6 days). He must have been on Greenwich Mean Time.

Twentieth-Century Records and Headlines

In 1910 the Touring Club of France sponsored a 100,000-km. race (62,137 miles). Dimitru Dan won easily because none of the other 199 competitors was able to finish.

In 1924 James Hocking at age 68 walked across the United States from New York to San Francisco in 75 days. He lived to 98 years and walked throughout his lifetime, covering over 200,000 miles. When he was 96, the Mark Twain Society elected him to honorary membership for his outstanding sports contribution. They had to make sure he wasn't just a flash in the pan.

In 1972 the Colorado Track Club went after the record for the 24-hour walk, relay fashion. The members of the team each did 17 miles sequentially, Jerry Brown leading the group with an average of 7 minutes 5 seconds per mile. The last man didn't quite have time to finish his hoped for 17 miles, and the total distance covered in the 24 hours was 162 miles and 275 yards.

Nonstop walking, also, was a recent challenge. The record for a nonstop walk fell four times in five years.

In 1971 in New Zealand, John Sinclair set a record of 230.80 miles.

In 1972 Richard Crawshaw, a restless, 54-year-old Member of Parliament, stayed afoot for 76 hours and 21 minutes to cover 255.84 miles. The *New York Times* reported the sleepless effort and quoted the walker near the end: "I'm beginning to feel a bit tired."

In New Mexico, Jesus "Jesse" Castañeda read about the Briton's feat and said to himself, "I can do better than that." His first two tries were almost disastrous. In his first attempt, the Southwest sun and heat struck him down after 18 hours and 78.5 miles. Five months later he walked for 90 hours 10 minutes through four rainstorms, covering 217.5 miles. At that point he fell asleep while walking and slumped to the ground. His support group could not get him awake enough to continue and so the record had to await a third try. Over the next five months Castañeda trained on the Albuquerque Academy track and got to know every inch of the surface. He would practice with his eyes closed until he could walk 2 miles without watching, hoping to be able to rest his eyes during his forthcoming effort. On March 16, 1973, the weather was perfect and Castañeda kept walking for 102 hours 59 minutes to complete 302 miles, a new record.

The British, good sports, honored Castañeda the following year. He met Crawshaw at a luncheon at the House of Commons and was introduced to Princess Margaret, who loved his sparkle.

But another Briton, Thomas Patrick Benson, decided that the record properly belonged in the Mother Country and on December 19, 1975, set out in the city of Preston's Moor Park to walk for almost 124 hours nonstop, completing 314 miles.

For a different record, John Merrill set out on January 3, 1978, to walk the entire coastline of Britain, about 7,000 miles in all. He endured all manner of weather, once nearly being blown off a seaside cliff. Ten months after starting out, Merrill was back to his starting point having experienced in that time "the most marvelous sense of remoteness."

In France there is an annual race that seems a little short compared to some of the other superhuman distances, but do not be deceived—it is one of the toughest. The Strasbourg to Paris race is 500 km., through villages and over country roads, without shelter from the weather. The competitors are given 72 hours to reach Paris. Those who complete the distance, rarely more than a handful, are judged on elapsed time. Those who don't make it are stopped at 72 hours and their distance walked is measured.

To give you an idea of what the 72-hour time limit means in a 500-km. race, let's take nice round numbers for average speed of walking:

At 5 miles per hour (12 minutes per mile), it would take 63 hours' walking time to cover the 315 miles. That leaves a total of nine hours over the three days for sleeping, eating, toilet, massage (if you have a good support crew), first aid (limited to blisters if you're lucky), and adding or subtracting clothes.

At 4 miles per hour (15-minute miles) you will owe the race officials 7 hours, not stopping at all.

In 1978 Paul Hendricks and his support crew from San Diego flew to France to be the first American ever to enter the race. Now there's a record that won't be broken.

That year there were 29 competitors—a small event, you might think—but the Europeans take the race seriously, some bringing along their personal physicians, physical therapists, coaches, cooks, and/or cheering sections. The support groups bring vans, campers, and all manner of re-adapted vehicles. Then there are all the spectators.

Paul Hendricks made a game attempt through the second day, but that night found him on a lonely country road under a pitch black sky—cold, tired, and drained of hope. He withdrew and was officially recorded as placing 21st. Only two of the 29 starters made it to Paris in the allotted time. Josey Simon from Luxembourg was timed in 66 hours 11 minutes and Serge Schneider of France in 69 hours 48 minutes. Neither of them came close to the record held by Robert Rinehard of Belgium of 63 hours 29 minutes.

It all seems hardly possible.

A Writer's Journal

Adam Nicolson is a latter-day writer-rambler of the English School. Like the early nineteenth-century writers, he walks not to set records but to take in the countryside and be part of each landscape he crosses. In accordance, he does not always stick to established byways, often climbing hills or crossing barrens when drawn in those directions. He will also change pace when the geography of the locale so dictates. Some terrain is meant for ambling, some for loping. There are beaches that invite dawdling just to watch the constant change on the face of the sea. There are also times that he will storm ahead for many miles, driven by the walking demon who has no sympathy for blistered feet.

Nicolson says that, for him, walking is an exercise in irresponsibility. He needs to make no decisions except to walk a little faster or a little slower. Walking deals with basics—going forward to where you are headed, or looking back to where you have been.

Geography and geology are basic to Nicolson's walks. He notes the brittleness of the limestone or the thickness of the peat. He imagines the thickness of an ancient glacier by judging the depth of the valley in which he is walking.

In France, Nicolson calls on geography to sanctify his love of good wines. Burgundy is one of his favorite tramping grounds, and he sees the wines of the region as a reflection of the soil he has walked upon. For him the wines are a kind of "bottled geography."

As a writer, Nicolson is well willing to share his walks. You can retrace his footsteps in his books *The National Trust Book of Long Walks in England, Scotland and Wales* (New York: Crown

Publishers, 1981) and *Long Walks in France* (New York: Crown Publishers, 1983).

Politicians

Politicians have always had to do a good deal of walking before election time. Campaigning requires them to be out among the voters—shaking hands, sampling ethnic foods at street fairs, just walking down Main Street. Once elected, they usually limit their walking to the hallways of the legislature.

One politician refused to be kept indoors. You may remember Harry S. Truman's daily walks. President Truman felt the need for the stimulation of walking out in the fresh air. The press quickly learned that the Chief Executive was more responsive on these walks than when he was closed in by the walls of a press conference room. Reporters who were in good shape took along their note pads and tried to keep pace with the President. By the end of his walk the one or two who were still with him were huffing and puffing whereas President Truman was fresh of breath and spirit. I think he enjoyed that unspoken advantage he had over the press.

Politics

Walking trails do not have a large or powerful constituency. No large government contracts are to be let, and no foreign troops are on our shores looking to trample the wildflowers along our historic trails. It is a wonder that any effort at all has been made to preserve our system of National Trails.

Fortunately there have been a few dedicated public servants in both Congress and in the Administration whose efforts have kept our National Trails from becoming overgrown and litter-strewn.

In 1965, President Lyndon B. Johnson, with the encouragement of the First Lady, asked Congress to draft legislation for the development of a National Trails System. It came to be known as the Natural Beauty Message. In concert with the President, Secretary of the Interior Stewart Udall asked the Bureau of Outdoor Recreation to undertake a study of trails and potential trails for inclusion in a national system.

Of course the Appalachian Trail Conference had been studying its own turf since 1925 and probably had accumulated some useful information. In the West, Californian Clinton C. Clark had an intimate knowledge of many high trails along the West Coast and by the 1940s envisioned a Pacific Crest Trail System from Canada to Mexico. In the government's own backyard, William O. Douglas knew about the beauty and serenity of the pathway along the Chesapeake and Ohio Canal. In 1954 the *Washington Post* suggested that a scenic parkway be built along the route, and Justice Douglas reacted by organizing a long walk along the canal from Cumberland, Maryland, to Washington, D.C., to show the *Post* what its proposal would destroy. The trail remained out of danger and later became the Potomac Heritage Trail.

The Department of the Interior went forward with its own official study. Secretary Udall provided leadership both administratively and in spirit. He was well-known as a conservationist and did not hesitate to personally dramatize the need to save the natural landscape treasures of the nation. Once, he arranged a press conference in the form of a walking tour along the Hudson River, then being despoiled by pollution. Another time he called attention to the valley of the Connecticut River.

The Department of the Interior was diligent and efficient, and the following year its 155-page incisive report was published under the title "Trails for America." The report recommended four trails as the mainframe of a National Trails System: the Appalachian Trail, the Pacific Crest Trail, the Continental Divide Trail, and the Potomac Heritage Trail. Several other trails were to be looked at for possible inclusion in the trails network.

In Congress, the legislation found strong sponsorship from Henry M. Jackson of Washington State, Gaylord Nelson of Wisconsin, and Peter Dominick of Colorado; and the National Trails Systems Act was signed into law on October 2, 1968. Quick work for the bureaucracy!

The Trails Act designated the Appalachian Trail and named 14 other trails to be studied for inclusion in the Trails System. The Continental Divide Trail and the Potomac Heritage Trail were among the 14.

The legislative process went forward with all deliberate speed under successive administrations, and in October of 1976, the National Trails System Act was amended to add another 8 trails to the previous 14 for study. The Daniel Boone Trail, stretching 350 miles from North Carolina to Kentucky, and the Florida Trail, 1,300 miles north from the Everglades, were 2 of the additional 8.

The momentum has continued and there are now over 100 National Recreation Trails, 8 National Scenic Trails, and 5 National Historic Trails. The Continental Divide Trail, the Potomac Heritage Trail, and the Florida Trail are all included in the National System.

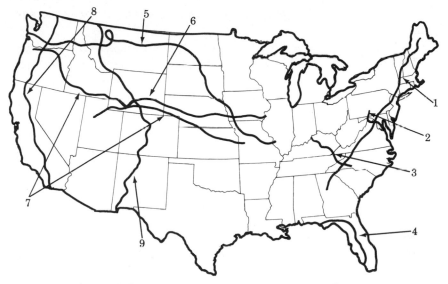

Some of the great trails of our National Trails System.
1. *The Appalachian Trail*
2. *The Potomac Heritage Trail*
3. *The Daniel Boone Trail*
4. *The Florida Trail*
5. *The Lewis and Clark Trail*
6. *The Mormon Pioneer Trail*
7. *The Oregon Trail*
8. *The Pacific Crest Trail*
9. *The Continental Divide Trail*

Families

One of the best incentives for continuing to walk for fitness is to have company, and what better company is there than someone you love.

In the community of race-walkers—those who compete and those who are in it solely for the exercise—there are a few parent-child combinations.

I have occasionally trained with my daughter Melissa. She at times may think I'm a mean old coach, but she accepts the help good naturedly and has developed good form and speed. I remember the bright spring day that we were each entered in a separate race in Central Park. The two races were arranged to follow one another, and so each of us was the personal cheerleader for the other. The encouragement must have worked, for we both won medals that day.

Another parent-child duo is Mayme and Nick Bdera. Surprise—Mayme is Nick's mother. Nick has made phenomenal strides in performance since his first race in Prospect Park one Thanksgiving Day. Now, four years later, Nick is in his mid-thirties and gives the best U.S. walkers something to worry about.

Mayme is in her sixties, still lean and energetic. She keeps up with most of the women 20 years younger and is cheered on by everyone. Sometimes I think Nick is a little jealous.

In another walking family, the Mimm kids deserve some sympathy. Their father, Bob, is a gentle soul, but put him in a pair of racing shoes and he becomes fierce. Bob was an Olympian in his younger days and has since set several age group records at several distances. Now in his sixties, he no longer can keep up with Randy or even Cliff. But Noreen, in her mid-twenties, is still no match for those experienced spring-steel legs. I, myself, am happy to be in a different age group and not have to compete directly with Bob Mimm.

Another former Olympian and force to be reckoned with is 6-foot 2-inch Dave Romansky. Most of Dave's race-walking activity nowadays is from the sidelines as a sharp-eyed coach for his two daughters. Denise has been getting stronger through her teens and is a determined racer, much as Dave was in the early 1970s. It is little Diana, however, that I remember best. My first Coney Island boardwalk race was also hers. She was only nine years old then and, along with a couple of oldsters, was given the maximum handicap. Diana left the starting line with an easy but rapid stride, but not with the determined Romansky look on her face. She just kept up her pace and never saw another walker's heels for the entire 10 miles. First place! Perhaps at nine years, a 10-mile race calls more for a relaxed style than determination.

After the race everyone made a great fuss over pretty little Diana, but she couldn't understand why. After all, she had only done her best.

In the outreaches of Brooklyn there is a new American, recently arrived from Eastern Europe. I do not know her name, having met her but once, but there is already a bond between us. She is a walker, too.

She and her small son walk around a neighborhood park most days of the week. She says she sees too many American kids whose free time is spent in front of "the tube," and she has decided her son will do something active and constructive with his free time.

While walking "for her son" she has noticed some positive changes in herself as well. By avoiding the afternoon programs on the idiot box, she has kept both her brain and her muscles from turning soft. An affluent new country was not going to exact its toll in atrophy if she could help it.

Power

Walking has recently gained a strong patron in the form of a former Mr. America. Steve Reeves, whose masculine image is beyond question, walks for exercise. Reeves' strides, long and forceful, are counterbalanced by an exaggerated arm swing. He calls the style "power walking." The motion is much like the classical form of cross-country skiing, and the metabolic benefits must be similar as well.

Reeves works out by power walking on his California ranch over all the ups and downs of the uneven terrain. He stays fit and looks the picture of a mature Hercules. Perhaps now, the ridicule factor in walking for exercise will be put to rest.

Chapter 11

Pleasures and Challenges

Walking, Not Just for Exercise

The curmudgeon-parodist Max Beerbohm said it would be all right with him if he never saw a buttercup or went out for a walk. He saw the brain and the soul in a struggle for control of the body. The soul commands the body to walk just for walking's sake, because "the mere fact of its doing so is a sure indication of nobility, probity, and rugged grandeur of character." The brain will not be a party to such "tomfoolery." If walking it is, then the brain puts all thinking on hold until the body rests easy in a cushioned chair again. Such was the gospel according to Max.

Well, Max Beerbohm was wrong. When it came to walking, he failed to consider the thinking process in all its depth. It may be true that walking quiets surface thought—the recall of facts, the expression of knowledge, and the straight line thinking of deductive reasoning—but walking favors more imaginative brain work. Walking makes for musing and free association. Walking loosens the thinking process so you can toss a knotty problem into the air and have it come down with all incongruities untangled. Perhaps because the "fact and logic" type of thinking is set aside during an hour's walk principles and paradoxes get attention. Straight line thinking is replaced by lateral and branched thinking, and unlikely connections are made. Even absurdities are well-considered and occasionally one will prove relevant to the matter at hand. Walking spurs the brain to work in the style of allowances.

That these very basic kinds of mentation occur during walking has captured the notice of many people, including some of history's famous thinkers. I will even grant the insight to runners. All types—writers, lawyers, salesmen, doctors, or machinists— who walk or run can use the hour of rhythmic, large muscle action to look past details and on to basics in their lives.

As to the famous:

Aristotle's disciples were called peripatetics because their philosophic talks took place as they walked around the Athenian countryside.

Samuel Taylor Coleridge often walked with a friend or two after dinner and brought to conversation dozens of subjects on which he offered observations, hypotheses, precedents, and beliefs. Had he sat down in his library with his friends he might have discussed only a single subject in stepwise sequence, but walking is more conducive to weblike patterns of thinking.

Albert Einstein, when one of his equations would not yield to the force of his genius, would go out for a long walk and think in metaphors, musing on unusual parallels between ordinary things. Often he would return with a new way of looking at the stubborn problem, and then the solution would become obvious to him.

You and I also have questions and concerns we want to resolve. They may not be so profound as those that nagged at Erasmus, Rousseau, Jefferson, or Freud (all serious walkers), but our problems are important to us. Perhaps through walking we can unburden our subconscious and free it to work on the sticky points in our lives.

Peace

A close cousin to free-flying thought is the sense of peace that comes with walking at a proper pace. The speed is the same for both mental attitudes—brisk, but less than all-out effort. It is a pace that you can set to automatic pilot.

Your walking hour will be yours alone. The rest of your daily environment will have to wait—people, places, and time schedules. During your workout, you will be sheltered from any inner storms of the day. It will be an hour of peace that you deserve.

Part of it is the rhythm you establish in your steps; part is the repeated contact with the earth. Also, there is the chance to use your eyes to see the elementary qualities of your surroundings— the shapes, the shapes within shapes, the darks and lights, the textures, colors, and contrasts. It is a return to basics.

Once you have experienced that inner calm, you will soon become addicted to it. Do not be alarmed. Interludes in daily routine, if taken in modest doses, can contribute to mental health—especially if the interlude is a walk for peace.

On Holiday

An hour's respite, three or four times a week, is the bread of our daily life. Once in a while we need a more festive diversion—a full day, an extended weekend, a week or two away. Wherever you live you can find walking tours whose primary purpose is not walking, but rather any of a wide variety of other interests.

In my home territory of New York, the Appalachian Mountain Club (New York-North Jersey Chapter) sponsors the following walks each year.

- Mushroom Walk on Blue Mountain
- Harriman Tree Hike—Hudson Highlands
- Hawks along the Hudson Tour
- Yoga and Meditation at Fire Island (beach walks included)
- Flowering Plants Workshop
- Nature Photography Workshop
- Herbal Medicine Workshop
- Silent Walk ("to see, hear, and experience pure delight in nature")
- Carol Singing and Gluwein at Pound Ridge (December)

In Gateway National Park, the Wildlife Refuge is a naturalist's paradise. The Park Rangers will give you all the information and help you can stand, and they will lead group walks to the best sites for the best sights.

In Stamford, Connecticut, there is a nature center where members and friends will meet on a winter evening for an "Owl Prowl." They come armed with tape recordings and flashlights, and they usually lure one or more of the night creatures into view.

Within reach of *your* home base, there are hiking clubs and nature centers that can start you off with walks to suit your fancy. You will find interest and kindred souls. All it takes is a lively stride.

Stepping into the Past

You may find the works of nature to be of less consequence than the works of man. If so, there are enough historic sites, landmarks, and districts to keep you busy for years.

The earliest settlements that you can visit in the United States are in Arizona. The Early Anasazi, the "basket makers," first built their villages on the canyon floor in A.D. 350. The Later Anasazi, the Pueblos, built wondrous cliff dwellings from A.D. 700 to 1300. Ruins of Antelope House, White House, Standing Cow, and several others can still be seen. Bring your walking shoes.

Diagonally across the nation, landmarks of the aboriginal peoples are less in evidence. Landmarks in the Northeast are largely devoted to the colonists, their revolution and nationhood.

At Concord, Massachusetts, you can follow the path of the redcoats' retreat when confronted by minutemen's rifles—from Old North Bridge past Meriam's Corner and down Battle Road to Lexington.

In Philadelphia it is more a tour of historic buildings: the American Philosophical Society (founded in 1768); Carpenters' Hall (meeting place of the First Continental Congress, 1774); Independence Hall (site of the signing of the Declaration of Independence, 1776); and Old City Hall (home of the Supreme Court until 1800).

Farther south another kind of revolution took place later on. At Kitty Hawk, North Carolina, the Wright brothers kept their heavier-than-air flying machine aloft under its own power for 12 seconds—a first. There is a national memorial where visitors can see a reproduction of the aircraft, the Wright brothers' camp that was used to prepare for the flights, and markers showing the take-off and landing sites. Figure on a little more walking than the 120 feet between the markers.

Out West, Dodge City, Kansas, will recall the frontier days when two-gun marshalls such as Bat Masterson and Wyatt Earp enforced an uneasy peace. You can walk down Front Street with its recreated saloons and visit Old Fort Dodge Jail—unarmed and comfortable in your walking shoes.

In the far West, Coloma, California, is the site of John Sutter's sawmill and the start of the gold rush.

Most cities across the nation have historical societies. Such organizations must number in the many hundreds. Any town that has been around since the turn of the century or before will be proud of its history and will have gathered together documents, photographs, and artifacts to form a collection for a historical society. Show even a passing interest to any society archivist and you will surely get an in-depth chronology and the offer of a tour.

In the northern reaches of Maine, the very small town of Greenville (year-round population, less than 2,000) stands at the southern end of Moosehead Lake, the last town before the wilds of the North Woods. The Moosehead Historical Society will take you on a tour of the Crafts-Sheridan House with its old country kitchen, its rooms of furnishings from bygone times, and exhibits of clothing from several ages of fashion. The region is rich in the history of the Abenaki and Penobscot tribes, the timber industry (still active), and canoe making (still being done by hand). To tour the town and its surroundings well, you will need to travel by plane, by boat, and on foot. The Historical Society is at your service.

If little Greenville can arrange a few tours, there must be many other towns in every state of the Union that can do it too.

Dateline, Europe

In Great Britain, walking traditions are even stronger than here in the colonies. The British walk to see the countryside and to relive their history, and they can arrange footpath holidays for widely divergent tastes.

In the Southwest, bordering on Bristol Channel, Exmoor National Park will take you along the Doone Valley to Dunkery Beacon and on to the ancient church at Stoke Pero. The Exmoor coast path climbs to the top of England's highest cliffs and heads east on a splendrous 12-mile ramble.

Across Bristol Channel, to the north, stands the state of Wales, Cymru to the Welsh. It is not an independent state, being part of Great Britain, but it is a state of independent being. In Wales, the names of places are strange to us and the land is almost as fascinating as the language. In the northeast, Snowdonia National Park will impress the Welsh landscape on your mind's eye. Snowdon Peak, Yr Wyddfa, rises to its full height of 3,560 feet only 10 miles from the sea and dominates the Gwynedd region. It is as if distances and heights were reduced to fit a smallish country and yet kept in proper proportions as a geographic parallel to the

Celtic ideals that have been part of Wales from pre-Roman times to the present.

In Scotland the topography is on a grander scale, and the walks can be as rugged and remote as they can be spectacular. In the Northern and Central Highlands, distances between towns and between roads are far spaced and the Scots tersely advise:

> *learn the use of map and compass,*
> *take windproofs and woolens,*
> *take torch and food.*

The Southern Highlands around beautiful Loch Lomond are less bleak and would be a good introduction to the Scottish countryside.

On the Continent, too, history is well defined. You can start with the time of the Impressionist School of painters. Many of the Dutch landscapes of Van Gogh can be seen both in the museums of Amsterdam and in three dimensions in the countryside. In France, you can walk through the compositions of Monet's paintings at Giverny and climb Cezanne's Mount Sainte-Victoire.

The Provence region of France where Cezanne worked goes back in history to the founding of Marseilles (Massalia) by the Phokaians of ancient Greece sometime about 600 B.C. Today, the region is one of sharp contrasts: stark and arid limestone ridges and vine-covered valleys, cities at once ancient and modern. There are many walks in and between the cities of Marseilles, Aix-en-Provence, and Saint Tropez where you can experience these contrasts.

A different past is well-preserved on the harsh Atlantic coast in Brittany. In the fifth century, when the southern Roman Empire was crumbling before the Ostrogoths, the Burgundians, and the Vandals, England and Scotland were invaded by the Angles, Saxons, and Jutes from what is today northern Germany and Denmark. The Celts who had inhabited the British Isles for a thousand years retreated into Wales or migrated to Brittany. Those who sailed south to Brittany retained their folkways there, and the culture that developed on that dour landscape is encountered wherever you walk.

History is more evident as you travel further east on the Mediterranean. In Italy, Roman history is with you everywhere—roads, aqueducts, buildings, columns, and amphitheaters. There are many forums, baths, and temples in varying states of preservation or ruin everyplace before your eyes. In Rome, itself, many structures are so close by that all you need is a guide book and comfortable walking shoes.

In Greece, history is written in large letters on the sun-whitened surface of the earth. A surprising number of names of islands and cities remain the same as in the golden age of Pericles. If you are familiar with ancient Greek coinage you will recognize the names and symbols of Melos, Thasos, Lesbos, Chios, Rhodes, and Aigina among the islands and Corinth, Argos, Larisa (Larissa, then), Chalcis, Thebes, and of course Athens among the cities. Mount Parnassus in its 8,000-foot glory looks down on the ruins of Apollo's and Athena's temples at Delphi in an atmosphere still charged with awe some 2,500 years later. In Athens and throughout Greece the genius and art of Greek architecture is ever present for your wonder.

Just Walking

If you walk through a country's landscapes and shorelines to record nature's grandeur in your memory, a guidebook can be a lens that brings all the elements into focus. In walking through history, a guidebook can help to place our ancestors in the context of the places visited.

In many lands, though, it is best to walk with no destination, to walk without expectation. Let your choice of trails, as you come to forks and intersections, bring discoveries to you. Let serendipity be your guide. The islands of the West Indies are especially good for discovery walking. The guidebooks of the Caribbean are more useful to sailors than to walkers anyway.

Two of the smaller islands come to mind as I sort through past holiday trips to the region. Bequia is a gemstone island in the Windward chain of the Grenadines. Bequia is renowned for its beaches along Admiralty Bay on the west and Friendship Bay on the east. But early one morning, it seemed like a good day for a walk in the hills along the spine of the island. There was no destination, just walking for its own sake and what might be discovered on the way. And discoveries there were. Looking out on the Atlantic from the high grassy plain there was a trio of small, open sailing boats that the natives had built by hand and used regularly for subsistence whaling. Farther on toward the upper side of Friendship Bay, a lone fisherman was silhouetted standing on the black rock shoals casting his line into the surf as the waves broke and washed over his feet. Higher in the hills I saw a scattered community of albino natives who, I later learned, had lived there for four generations.

Montserrat is another smallish island for walking. It is a volcanic island with only two hard-to-find sandy beaches. The fascinations of the island are in its Irish heritage and its rugged tropical interior. The Galway Soufrière with its boiling sulphur springs is worth a 5-mile hike into the mountains. But just as fascinating as the works of nature was the human work that I came upon in Plymouth, the capital of the island. One day while walking wherever my legs would take me, I was stopped by the sight of the shoe repairman sitting in the doorway of his home/shop, marking the outlines for new soles on a large sheet of cowhide. He took special pains to waste as little leather as possible, drawing the outlines like an artist. He was an elderly man doing his work with the attention and precision of handwork that grew from a pride in his craft.

Rush Hours and Other Apoplexy

Coming home from a holiday abroad into J.F.K. Airport, I always feel a pull on that niche in my brain that keeps a concentration of hometown magnetic particles. As wonderful as an interlude in a charming or exotic country may be, I always feel a glow on seeing that familiar skyline as the plane approaches the airport.

The good feeling generally lasts for a full half hour until I hit the steel-on-wheels wall of traffic on the parkway going home.

The plague of cars is becoming ever more rampant, creating a morbidity of spirit in our cities. There used to be a radio program called "Life with Luigi" that put a finger on the essence of the matter. The program began with Luigi writing a letter to his mother in the old country. On one show Luigi's letter opened:

"Dear Mama mia,

"Everyone here in the United States is so busy, always rushing. They even have a special hour for rushing. . . ." And so we do. Ultimately, it is a question of moving people from point A to point B in the most efficient way. Cars represent the worst kind of transport. Not only do they move fewer people per hour than other vehicles, but their engines also poison the air between point A and point B.

In terms of efficiency in moving the maximum number of people per hour, there is a tie between trains and walking shoes. Lewis Mumford, who is an ardent defender of the "footwalker," estimates that before the invention of the internal combustion engine, about 50,000 people per hour used to pass over London Bridge on their way to work. Mumford estimates rail transportation to be about the same 50,000 per hour. Cars are good (good?) for 5,000 people per hour assuming no traffic jams.

Walking as a means of transportation ought to be a priority with city planners. Most people who either drive to work or take public transportation will accept a door to door time of anything under an hour. In the city a fairly close-by job may take the better part of an hour. A 3-mile distance between home and office, what with traffic delays or having to wait for buses or trains, can take up to 45 minutes. These same 3 miles on foot can take the same 45 minutes.

This was exactly my own experience a few years ago. At that time my office was 3 miles from home, but no single bus line ran between the two points; it was necessary to transfer from one bus to another. I would often travel by car, and occasionally I would take the two buses. Waiting for both buses plus actual riding time generally added up to 50 minutes.

It took an unexpected snowstorm one January to place my transportation choices in perspective. I had to come to the office by bus in a sprinkling of light snow. It snowed throughout the day, and in the afternoon was especially heavy. By 4:00 P.M., wheels were slipping and spinning under otherwise motionless vehicles. Taxicab service was virtually nonexistent, and the few buses that were on the road were stuck behind cars that were stuck in the snow. I was going to have to hoof it.

After a few blocks, I established a comfortably fast cadence, and before I knew it, I was walking down my own block. Door to door took 48 minutes. The snow had made for slower going, but then there was no traffic to wait for at cross streets. I could walk the distance—snow or no—in less time than it took to go by bus! It was a revelation.

I decided I would time the walk again, this time on dry pavement, and also check out bicycling time. Brisk walking took

45 minutes, and cycling—stop lights and traffic included—took 17 minutes.

Thereafter, I rarely took bus transportation; I rode my bicycle fairly often and I walked. Car use was for the days I would have to travel beyond the office.

Beating the traffic is a matter of changing how we think about getting from place to place. If we could stop thinking of cars as the only way to get around, car travel would quickly diminish in our society.

Ring-a-levio Security Patrol

When I was a kid growing up in Brooklyn, there were empty lots, few cars, and little formal recreation. The streets were our playgrounds. We got together for punchball, stickball, and ring-a-levio. I suppose our games were a noisy annoyance to the adults who lived there, but our presence did help to create a sense of neighborhood.

Nowadays, I don't see much stickball or ring-a-levio, nor do I see the integrity of neighborhoods that I knew as a kid. What can be done? We can recapture the neighborhoods by our presence on the streets. Enough eyes and ears open to the sights and sounds of the now faceless places will create a good old-fashioned sense of neighborhood. Walkers can accomplish what we once did with our games.

In the Running

Ring-a-levio and box ball players may be all but extinct, but there has been an explosive growth in other sports. In the contagion of enthusiasm, many new athletes go at their new found fun all-out. Intensity and/or duration of effort are extreme even if these athletes are only weekend warriors. Unfortunately, in their pursuit of the gusto, they often become injured along the way.

Enter: walking. The reality of the world is that some folks will choose something other than walking as their primary sport. How unwise. Other athletes can benefit from walking as a secondary activity. Walking can serve even marathoners well, even professional football players.

Walking uses all the muscles of the legs and also gives some work to the muscles of the trunk and arms and shoulders. Walking provides a good general tone-up for almost any other sport and is especially valuable as an adjunct to leg sports. More specifically, walking strengthens the muscles of the front of the lower leg and the muscles of the back of the upper leg (the hamstrings). These are the very muscles that make trouble for runners, hobbling them with shin splints or hamstring tears.

Several professional football players have recurrent hamstring problems that keep them out of action several games each season. Hamstring grief seems to be endemic to the New York Jets, especially the defensive line. As a loyal Jet fan with a sports medicine background, I offer walking as the hamstring cure. I can imagine the response I will get to the suggestion that these great creatures take up walking. Something like, "Real men don't eat quiche, either." Yet, some of their colleagues, all equally large, have developed expertise in such un-macho pursuits as music and gardening. The kind of walking needed to strengthen the hamstrings would not be "tiptoeing through the tulips," but rather long, powerful strides with a strong pulling motion from the moment of heel strike, a kind of brute-force walking.

In runners, whether their distances are 100 yards or 10,000 meters, about 50 percent of them come up short with shin splints. Walkers, even competitive race-walkers, rarely have shin splints. Their lower leg muscles and tendon attachments are strong from the motions of the heel-and-toe sport that runners need.

Another sport that would benefit from walking is cross-country skiing. The strong "kick" of Nordic skiing needs strong muscles of the back and buttocks as well as strong hamstrings. The two sports are symbiotic. Indeed, Ray Sharp, who set a world's record for the 1-mile walk (5:46.2 and never off the ground), uses cross-country skiing for wintertime training.

Cross-country skiing has become a tradition with the Metropolitan Racewalkers, too. Each winter the club schedules a weekend in Vermont and charters a bus for the event. It is not really a training weekend but rather a one of good fellowship in a sport not all that different from walking. The weekend attracts more walkers each year, and I think it must be the similarities between the two sports.

Help Wanted: Fitness

Walking will prepare you not only for play, but for work as well. You will have a higher energy level, greater patience, and less anxiety—all important factors in doing better work in the market-place.

Two occupations are more specific in physical requirements: fire fighting and police work. Applicants must be healthy (that is, free of disease) and well-conditioned as well. They must be possessed of strength, speed, and stamina; and women applicants are given no privileges.

A few articles have appeared in the sports medicine literature concerning fitness in fire fighters and the appropriateness of the physical performance examination to actual fire fighting tasks.

A few articles have also appeared in the newspapers concerning the design of the tests and whether they were meant to keep women out of the firehouses. It was getting pretty serious between the sexes, with all the writs, suits, and public statements flying, until one woman applicant in a stroke of spontaneity demonstrated her quickness and strength by throwing her 6-foot 2-inch, 185-pound attorney over her shoulder in a "fireman's carry." The judge was suitably impressed, and both sides at this writing are working out a test that will be fair to the women and still hold the department to high standards of performance. The new tests that are being devised are based on several of the sports medicine findings that have been reported.

Stamina and aerobic capacity seem to be more important than strength. Aerobic capacity is especially important when the atmosphere at the site of a fire contains toxic gases. Resistance to fatigue, another face of aerobic capacity, is vital for maintaining alertness and a level of arduous activity over several hours.

The International Association of Fire Chiefs is in accord. Members know that more fire fighters are lost to heart attacks than to fires.

The fire fighters need fitness urgently. The chiefs should sound a Klaxon horn to start programs that can be maintained through each professional's career. Walking is the one exercise program that will bring fitness into the firehouse with no risk of injury to the muscles that must do the rescue work.

The police are in as much need of stamina as are fire fighters. The policewomen I interviewed expressed pride in being able to run up long flights of stairs in a specified time and to drag a 125-pound mannequin down a hallway. After passing the test they all felt the sense of self-confidence so necessary to good police work.

PLEASURES AND CHALLENGES 157

Sow Ears and Pig Tales

In the early 1970s, a Masters track meet was held at Stroudsburg, Pennsylvania. It was the Eastern Masters Championship, and men over 40 came from many states from Maine to Florida.

The sprint events were about to start when a group of women carrying placards marched up to the officials' table.

"Why aren't women included in the event?" they demanded to know. The response of the officials left the women dumbfounded.

"Welcome," said the officials. "We have been trying to get women to participate."

The women were invited to put on running shoes and enter any events they wished. Three of them (all in their thirties) signed up for the 1 mile run, but they seemed hesitant at being included in the 50–59-year-old men's section.

The mile went off, and the three women rapidly fell behind, eventually finishing last in a field of more than a dozen runners. The women had not prepared themselves to race if their protest succeeded.

Today women are making spectacular gains in sports. Younger women are closing the gap between men's and women's world records in virtually every sport. Masters women are now giving their brother athletes a run for their money. In road racing, men and women run or walk the same course at the same time, and in race-walking there are more women participants than men.

When I enter an occasional walking race I am usualy in a lone zone of competition among the men of my age group. The very best men are too fast, and the rest are behind me. My closest competitor is usually Dorothy Kelley, who sets a torrid pace for both of us, warm weather or cold. She and I are less than four years apart in age and even closer in performance. We are not in competition for medals or trophies—there are always separate men's and women's awards—but for the enjoyment of one-to-one racing that spurs us to better individual performance. The competition is always good natured and engenders mutual respect and friendship.

A Step beyond Fitness

Robert Ardrey, the playwright-ethologist, in his book *The Territorial Imperative* (New York: Atheneum, 1966), delineated three major psychological drives in the human species: (1) ego, (2)

A demonstration of strong racing form.

security, and (3) stimulation. Man needs a little excitement in life, and the fire of competition in athletics can satisfy the drive of stimulation.

If competition becomes all-consuming so that it directs your life, then it is not healthful for mind or body. This kind of personal pressure is characteristic of a type A personality, a high risk factor in the coronary heart disease profile.

Below the professional level, sports competition should be less than nth power serious if we are to keep fun in our games. Losing does not mean disgrace or insolvency. Winning, as an amateur, does not mean great fame or fortune.

In the worlds of business and industry, of government and academe, the sharks, hawks, and tigers play for high stakes. Losing can bring depression; winning can bring grandiosity.

Walking competition has several safeguards against taking yourself too seriously. Race-walkers are limited in their stylistic freedom by the I.A.A.F. (International Amateur Athletic Federation) rules. There are only two rules, but they are absolute. First, walkers must keep continuous contact with the ground. The advancing foot must contact the ground before the rear foot leads. No running ("lifting") is allowed. Second, the leg in contact with the ground must be straightened at the knee when in the vertical support position. Walking in the Groucho Marx style ("creeping") is not allowed.

In every race-walk event, the competitors must walk "fairly" or they will be disqualified by the judges. The walkers must watch their step throughout the course, for the judges check for violations with stealth and cunning. They hide behind trees and use bicycles and field glasses to apprehend the man or woman who breaks the rules. The enforcement of the rules keeps the walkers on the straight and narrow and even confers a bit of humility.

The walking races that are held are like a family affair. Old and young, male and female, all start together on the same course. Sometimes whole families are in a race together—parents and children, brothers and sisters. The former Olympian, Bob Mimm, is usually accompanied by one or two of his children. They are all tough competitors.

In a sanctioned race the field may number as few as a dozen or may be over a hundred. There may be a personal rivalry here and there, but overall, only two or three have a chance at first place. The rest of the competitors know they have no chance of winning, and so they have no fear of losing. They are concerned about their own performance as measured in minutes and seconds rather than by overall place.

Race-walking also encourages the personal qualities of discipline and realistic self-appraisal. Discipline is necessary to hold to the rules at every stride. Self-assessment as to form is needed in order to develop a fluid and efficient motion and to continue improving.

Race-walking can sharpen your wits in terms of tactics and strategy. It can even bring out a touch of creativity.

First assess your strengths. If you have the speed for a finishing "kick," there are a couple of strategies for winning in a psychological duel with a close competitor:

1. In a 3-mile race, for example, stay shoulder to shoulder for the middle mile. At the last mile, slow your speed so imperceptibly that your rival does not notice it and stays even with you. In the last stretch, perhaps 150 yards from the finishing line, turn on the steam.

2. If you cannot quite hold your rival's pace, do not try to stay so close that you remain a threat. Then, he or she may ease up enough for you to hold the same pace and still stay within striking distance. In the last half mile, close the gap and then sprint home over the last 150 yards.

Assess your rival's weaknesses. If he/she is the nervous type stay close on his/her heels to encourage worry. Apprehension saps energy and endurance. Do not attempt to take the lead until near the end of the race when you can hold a faster pace through the finish line.

I remember one cool Sunday that I felt mischievous. I put on a warm-up suit that had a couple of A.A.U. Masters Championship patches prominently displayed and set out for Central Park, where a 5-km. race was to be held. After arriving at the park and signing in, I did a couple of fast-paced warm-ups.

At the start of the race I stayed close to the leaders, men in their early twenties, for about a quarter mile. It was a mad dash pace. Two competitors in my own age group must have thought that I was possessed by some mercurial spirit, and they just settled into their own comfortable rhythms. My early pace slowed, of course, but my two rivals did not realize that they had a chance to catch me until midway through the race. One did pass me after the 2-mile mark, but by then he could not gain much of a lead. I stayed close until the last 100 yards and then opened up with a long, fast stride and beat him to the finish line.

The best fun came when I mentioned to him at the award ceremony that it was too bad there weren't any championship patches being awarded.

"It would have been nice," I said, "to have a championship patch that I won in race-walking to go with the two that I had previously won for pole vaulting."

If an occasional touch of competition appeals to you, race-walking shares all the advantages and benefits of brisk walking as outlined in the Walking Program. My advice is to go for it. You can find good material on technique in Julian Hopkins' book *Race Walking* (London: British Amateur Athletic Board, 1976), Martin Rudow's *Race Walking* (Mountain View, Calif.: World Publications, 1975), and more recently Howard Jacobson's *Racewalk to Fitness* (New York: Simon and Schuster, 1980).

Nowadays you can find a few race-walkers wherever there are runners in numbers. Just sidle up to one who looks natural at the sport and you will get aid and encouragement. You can get more formal help from some of the sports organizations that are devoted just to race-walking or that have race-walking divisions.

The Walkers Club of America is old and venerable, going back to 1911. Recently, the W.C.A. has been increasing the pace of its activities and now has chapters in many cities across the nation. In the New York metropolitan area it is the New York Walkers Club

Mort Malkin in his warm-up suit with championship patches.

with Central Park as its home base. You can get in touch with the W.C.A. at 445 East 86th St., New York, NY 10128.

The Athletic Congress (T.A.C.) has a race-walking committee that sponsors many national championships. Its address is P.O. Box 120, Indianapolis, IN 46206.

The Masters Sports Association has clubs in many cities, and each local club has a race-walking division. New York, Philadelphia, and Washington, D.C. are strong on continuing athletics and race-walking in particular. The New York Masters Sports Club is at 77 Prospect Place in Brooklyn, NY 11217.

There are several race-walking clubs ready and willing to provide instruction and company. My own club is the Metropolitan Racewalkers, whose headquarters (and pasta parties) are at 36 West 20th St., New York, NY 10011.

The Island Track Club trains on the back roads of Long Island. You can reach coach Gary Westerfield at Box 440, Smithtown, NY 11787.

New Jersey's Shore A.C. includes former Olympians Bob Mimm and Elliott Denman and is at 28 North Locust Ave., West Long Branch, NJ 07764.

Then there are the Potomac Valley Striders, the New Jersey Striders, the Central Massachusetts Striders, and the gang from the Niagara Association AAU.

Henry Laskau, the dean of American race-walkers, lives in Coconut Creek, Florida, and coaches any and all race-walkers within reach.

There is even a small monthly magazine, *The Ohio Racewalker,* published by former Olympian Jack Mortland at 3184 Summit St., Columbus, OH 43202.

Race-walking is best approached by viewing the sport as an extension of brisk walking rather than as a new complexity of contortions. The motion should be natural and rhythmic, not forced. Try not to try too hard. Watch others who have good form and learn by "wholes."

Race-walking is a technique event that is challenging and satisfying. It's worth trying. Perhaps we'll meet at a race sometime.

Nutrition Counsel

Walking, race-walking or brisk walking, can magically make for better nutrition. It is not by breathing in more vitamins from the air or by spontaneous generation of minerals in your working muscles. Rather it is a matter of being able to increase the total amount of food in your diet, the total number of calories per day or per week.

Let's take an example and round off the numbers. Say that you are walking 4 miles, four times a week, fairly fast. Say that you are (1) directly burning 2,000 extra calories for the week just by the physical work performed and (2) increasing your general metabolic caloric consumption by another 2,000 calories per week. The exercise will increase your requirements of vitamins, minerals, amino acids, etc., by only minimal amounts, and only for a few nutrient factors at that. Energy requirements, however, will be increased by 4,000 calories per week and by taking in food to supply that energy you will increase nutrients as well. That assumes, of course, that the extra food does not contain just empty calories.

Four thousand calories represents a generous amount of soup, salad, fruit, vegetables, and protein sources (meat, fish, etc.), and probably would leave room for a couple of chocolate truffles. Just think of all the extra vitamins, essential amino acids, essential fatty acids, macro-minerals, and trace elements you could absorb in those 4,000 calories.

Even if you wanted to lose a little weight at the same time and you increased your total of weekly calories by 2,000, you would more than make up for the very slight increase in nutrients that moderate exercise demands.

Walking for fitness will lead to health by better nutrition as well as by exercise per se. And if you enjoy the taste of good food, well prepared, as I do, you will appreciate the room you will have for the extra dollop of calories.

There are other perks that come along with fitness. In Chapter 5, I mentioned how one friend solved the New York midtown parking problem with his walking skills. An insurance agent I know has told me that a select few companies are giving a discount on life insurance premiums for those who are enrolled in fitness programs. I, myself, once put my walking endurance to good use in a walkathon for the cause of peace.

As you breeze down the path of fitness you will come upon a windfall that will be special for you.

References

Ardrey, Robert. *The Territorial Imperative.* New York: Atheneum, 1966.

Butwin, David. "Getting Away: Take a Hike." *The Physician and Sportsmedicine,* May 1984, pp. 155–58.

Davis, J. A., M. H. Frank, B. J. Whipp, and K. Wasserman. "Anaerobic Threshold Alterations Consequent to Endurance Training in Middle-Aged Men." *Medicine and Science in Sports,* vol. 11, no. 1, 1979, p. 96.

Davis, Paul O., Charles O. Dotson, and D. Laine Santa Maria. "Relationship between Simulated Firefighting Tasks and Physical Performance Measures." *Medicine and Science in Sports and Exercise,* vol. 14, no. 1, 1982, pp. 65–71.

Hopkins, Julian. *Race Walking.* London: British Amateur Athletic Board, 1976.

Jacobson, Howard. *Racewalk to Fitness.* New York: Simon and Schuster, 1980.

Morgan, William P. "Affective Beneficence of Vigorous Physical Activity." *Medicine and Science in Sports and Exercise,* vol. 17, no. 1, 1985, pp. 94–100.

Morris, Jan. *The Matter of Wales.* New York: Oxford University Press, 1984.

Murphy, Patrick. "Life Insurers Offer Health Incentives." *The Physician and Sportsmedicine,* March 1984, p. 15.

Ransford, Charles P. "A Role for Amines in the Antidepressant Effect of Exercise: A Review." *Medicine and Science in Sports and Exercise,* vol. 14, no. 1, 1982, pp. 1–10.

Rogers, Cindy Christian. "Firing Up for Fitness." *The Physician and Sportsmedicine,* April 1984, pp. 134–42.

Rozek, Michael. "Walking Tall." *Physician's Sportslife,* May/June 1985, p. 20.

Rudow, Martin. *Racewalking.* Mountain View, Calif.: World Publications, 1975.

Sheehan George. "How Important Is the Clock?" *The Physician and Sportsmedicine,* February 1984, p. 47.

Weber, F., R. J. Barnard, and D. Roy. "Effects of an Intensive, Short-Term Nutrition and Exercise Program on Individuals Age 70 and Older." *Medicine and Science in Sports and Exercise,* vol. 14, no. 2, 1982, pp. 179–80.

Young, R. John. "Effect of Regular Exercise on Cognition and Personality." Abstracts of the 25th Annual Meeting of American College of Sports Medicine, vol. 10, no. 1, 1978, p. 51.

Walker's Journal

Use the space at the top of the page for each week to write in the time (or distance) and pace of the workouts for that week. Notice that frequency is not negotiable. You must walk three or four times per week.

Use the following schedule to determine time and pace for each week, starting with whatever week you actually begin your walking program.

First week: Walk for 10 minutes at a leisurely pace.

Second week: Walk briskly for 15 minutes.

Third week. Walk briskly for 22 minutes.

Fourth week: Walk briskly for 33 minutes.

Fifth week: Walk at a steady pace for 45 minutes.

Sixth week: Walk briskly for 45 minutes.

Seventh week: Walk at a steady pace for 60 minutes.

Eighth week: Walk briskly for 60 minutes.

All following weeks: Walk 4 miles in 1 hour or better (4 mph).

Under each date there is a square in which you can check off your workout. You can also write in comments on how you felt and who or what you saw, note routes and distances, and make promises wherever you wish. It's your journal.

January

Walk three or four times a week.

Pace: Pace:

Time: Time:

1 ☐ *Let's start the New Year with just an easy workout. No, not the first thing in the morning, but you can pull yourself together by noon.*	**8** ☐
2 ☐	**9** ☐ *So it snowed yesterday. Wear mukluks instead of walking shoes, but work out. You may reduce your time by one-third.*
3 ☐ *Today, it's back to your proper workout schedule. Keep up the resolve.*	**10** ☐
4 ☐	**11** ☐ *If you are plagued by a cholesterol problem, most doctors will tell you that walking can be a strong ally in controlling it.*
5 ☐ *A regular walking program is as much about losing inches as about losing pounds. A slimmer waist is worth walking for.*	**12** ☐
6 ☐	**13** ☐
7 ☐	**14** ☐ *When walking in boots in the snow, use a shorter stride and pull from the heel (forward foot) rather than to push off from the toe.*

January

Walk three or four times a week.

Pace: Pace:

Time: Time:

15 ☐ *When the wind-chill factor is below zero, wear at least three good layers, including a turtleneck. Don't forget hat and gloves.*	**22** ☐
16 ☐	**23** ☐ *A cinnamon stick and a teaspoon of brandy will make the hot tea taste even better.*
17 ☐ *When you're standing, there should be a minimum of 1/2 inch between the end of your shoe and the end of your longest toe.*	**24** ☐
18 ☐	**25** ☐
19 ☐ *On a blustery day, it's nice to come back from a workout to a cup of hot tea. Trade favors with some good-hearted soul who might have it ready for you.*	**26** ☐ *Think how nice it is not to have to worry about sunburn.*
20 ☐	**27** ☐
21 ☐	**28** ☐ *Anyone who can walk does not have to be fat.*

January

Walk three or four times a week.

Pace:

Time:

Pace:

Time:

29 ☐	**31** ☐
30 ☐ *A January thaw? Here's your chance to wear lighter clothing when you go out to walk, but be aware that 42°F is not shorts and singlet weather.*	

February

Walk three or four times a week.

Pace:

Time:

Pace:

Time:

1 ☐	**5** ☐ *If you walk frequently on a regular basis, you are doing something positive to aid in your body's most efficient use of carbohydrates.*
2 ☐ *Oh, did the groundhog go back into his burrow without doing a workout? Did you ever see a groundhog that wasn't fat, lazy, and short-lived?*	**6** ☐
3 ☐	**7** ☐ *By now you really enjoy walking and look forward to each outing. As you become stronger, imagine yourself training for competition in nice, warm Mexico. Set goals.*
4 ☐ *Gerontologists agree that people who exercise live longer. You might walk yourself into the charmed circle of centenarians.*	**8** ☐

February

Pace:

Pace:

Time:

Time:

9 ☐	**16** ☐
10 ☐ *Does some family member kid you about walking for fitness? Pay no attention to such an attitude. Remember, you are in it for you.*	**17** ☐ *Be sure the widest part of your foot and the widest part of your walking shoe coincide. If they don't, you have the wrong shoes for your feet.*
11 ☐	**18** ☐
12 ☐ *Imagine the hills in your workout path to be like those outside of Springfield, Illinois, where Abe Lincoln walked to clarify his thoughts. You can do it, too.*	**19** ☐ *Prolonged inactivity leads to calcium drain from the bones. Walking movement helps to return this mineral to the bones.*
13 ☐	**20** ☐
14 ☐ *Today is a good day for a walk with your sweetheart.*	**21** ☐
15 ☐	**22** ☐ *If the weather is discouraging, remind yourself of Washington's men marching for days to Valley Forge. You're just out for an hour. You'll soon be home!*

February

Walk three or four times a week.

Pace: Pace:

Time: Time:

23 ☐	**26** ☐
24 ☐	**27** ☐ *No, the warm-up is not counted toward workout time. Build an extra five minutes into your customary schedule.*
25 ☐ *Don't forget to warm up before hitting your workout pace. You never get beyond the need for these few minutes of preparation.*	**28** ☐

March

Walk three or four times a week.

Pace: Pace:

Time: Time:

1 ☐ *Distance walking is no novelty. In 1861, Edward P. Weston walked from Boston to Washington, D.C., a distance of 478 miles, in 208 hours.*	**4** ☐
2 ☐	**5** ☐
3 ☐ *Walking is the best warm-up for walking.*	**6** ☐ *Hang in there; spring will be here soon. You're through the worst of it. Don't let your resolve melt now. Stick to the schedule.*

March

Pace:

Time:

Walk three or four times a week.

Pace:

Time:

7
☐

14
☐
Consider your workout as a political statement. By walking, you are registering your opposition to the internal combustion engine.

8
☐
Not in the mood for a workout? Just go out for a 5-minute warm-up. The improved circulation to the brain may energize you.

15
☐

9
☐

16
☐

10
☐

17
☐
Wear your green headband on St. Patrick's Day. Are you Irish? Sure and begorra!— in spirit, if not in ancestry. Aren't "brogans" the Irish walking shoes?

11
☐
William Wordsworth composed much of his poetry while walking. When he died at age 80, he had walked an estimated 185,000 miles.

18
☐

12
☐
Bones respond to exercise in avoiding osteoporosis. One-fourth of the body's bones are in the feet ... get walking!

19
☐
Walk to get fit for golf or tennis or other sports, but don't depend on sports alone to keep you fit.

13
☐

20
☐

March

Pace:

Time:

Walk three or four times a week.

Pace:

Time:

21 ☐	Is some errand that you might ordinarily drive to really close enough for walking? Walk there leisurely, even though it isn't your regular walking day.	**27** ☐	On gusty days, when walking against the wind, take shorter strides; with the wind, stretch out into a longer stride.
22 ☐		**28** ☐	
23 ☐		**29** ☐	Walking is in fashion, but in terms of shoes the right type counts more than the right style. Be comfortable in well-fitted walking shoes.
24 ☐		**30** ☐	
25 ☐	A windy day is no excuse to skip a workout. Let the wind at your back help you to accomplish your mission.	**31** ☐	
26 ☐			

April

Pace:

Time:

Walk three or four times a week.

Pace:

Time:

1 ☐	*You can't fool your body with only one or two workouts a week. It will know you're not serious about fitness and won't change its lazy metabolic ways.*
8 ☐	
2 ☐	*In Austria, an unidentified man walked 40 miles on his hands. You'll have a wonderful workout if you walk just one-tenth of that distance upright!*
9 ☐	*A 15-minute walk of moderate but steady pace calms anxiety tensions better than tranquilizers.*
3 ☐	
10 ☐	*With your new outfit and wondrous form, imagine yourself as the focus of a story in* Sports Illustrated. *Walk like a champion.*
4 ☐	*Are you due for a reward for keeping to your workout schedule? How about a new sweat shirt in daffodil yellow? It's the right season.*
11 ☐	
5 ☐	
12 ☐	*Maybe a cover photo would be better than a story. Remind yourself of the sacrifice and dedication that got you this far. Resolve to keep at it.*
6 ☐	
13 ☐	
7 ☐	*How about a hyacinth pink sweat shirt? Or tulip red? Just choose any color that makes you happy. Buy a couple.*
14 ☐	

April

Pace:

Time:

Walk three or four times a week.

Pace:

Time:

15 ☐	**22** ☐
16 ☐ *For quick relief of leg or foot muscle cramps while you are lying down, stand firmly on the flat of the affected foot and press it down as hard as possible.*	**23** ☐
17 ☐	**24** ☐ *Today is Secretaries Day. Secretaries and bosses who go out to restaurants to celebrate might eat too much. An evening workout is in order.*
18 ☐ *It has to rain sometime, and April is the traditional month for it. You can walk tomorrow if the rain is too heavy today. But a light rain is no excuse.*	**25** ☐
19 ☐	**26** ☐ *Fatties who choose vigorous exercise routines tend to give up. The people who stick it out—and lose weight—are walkers.*
20 ☐	**27** ☐
21 ☐ *Stay away from auto traffic when you walk. Cars are out to get you. Even if they don't score a direct hit, they'll poison the air.*	**28** ☐ *You are a diligent walker. You deserve a reward. During today's walk decide what it will be. Don't stint.*

April

Pace:

Time:

Walk three or four times a week.

Pace:

Time:

29 ☐

30 ☐ *In the average lifetime, a person will walk about 125,000 miles—five times around the world!*

May

Pace:

Time:

Walk three or four times a week.

Pace:

Time:

1 ☐ *It may be May, but it can still be cool. Cool is not so bad, but watch out for cool-wet or cool-windy weather.*

6 ☐

2 ☐

7 ☐

3 ☐

8 ☐ *You've already worn out two pairs of walking shoes? Congratulations! Think of it this way: buying shoes is cheaper than paying medical bills.*

4 ☐ *Mark your calendar for the day you started a walking program. It will be a day to celebrate for the rest of your life.*

9 ☐

5 ☐ *So the trees in your park are not sequoias. Maples and ornamental cherry trees make oxygen, too. Learn to identify the types of trees you pass.*

10 ☐ *Only mothers are excused from working out on Mother's Day. A mother whose gifts include an exercise outfit will probably want to walk anyway!*

May

Pace:

Time:

Walk three or four times a week.

Pace:

Time:

11 ☐ *If you're one of the many people with a hammertoe, don't buy shoes with a seam that runs over that toe.*	**18** ☐
12 ☐	**19** ☐ *If your disposition is something less than charming due to the day's happenings, a brisk walk will help you cool off while you firm up.*
13 ☐	**20** ☐
14 ☐	**21** ☐ *If you walk in shorts and a T-shirt today, watch out for a chill afterward due to a damp shirt and a cool breeze. Cover up to prevent a cold.*
15 ☐ *A dish of berries or fresh fruit is refreshing after a workout. Get them ready before you leave so they're waiting for you to enjoy.*	**22** ☐
16 ☐	**23** ☐
17 ☐	**24** ☐ *A good race-walker's stride measures from 10 to 16 inches more than the average walker and covers a mile in about 12 minutes.*

May

Pace:

Time:

Walk three or four times a week.

Pace:

Time:

25 ☐ *Walking, a moderate exercise, increases sex hormone levels. Your mate deserves to know this.*

29 ☐

26 ☐

30 ☐ *There will be at least one nice day this Memorial Day weekend. It's been arranged. Even if you go out of town, you can find an attractive place for a workout.*

27 ☐

31 ☐

28 ☐ *Most insomniacs would find themselves nodding off at bedtime effortlessly if they were taking brisk walks on a regular basis.*

June

Pace:

Time:

Walk three or four times a week.

Pace:

Time:

1 ☐

3 ☐ *Victims of heart attacks are routinely advised to embark on a regular, carefully planned walking program.*

2 ☐

4 ☐

June

Walk three or four times a week.

Pace:

Pace:

Time:

Time:

5 ☐	*Don't forget to stretch after every workout. Even if you think you don't need it, it's important to set a good example for those who do.*
6 ☐	
7 ☐	
8 ☐	*If you see a runner pull up short with a hamstring spasm, show the poor soul how to stretch as you do. This kindness might make a convert for the "safe sport."*
9 ☐	
10 ☐	*Some people have walked across the entire United States—surely you can walk around your neighborhood.*
11 ☐	

12 ☐	
13 ☐	*Stopping for a few seconds for a drink of water does not count as an interruption in your workout. Stopping for coffee at a diner does.*
14 ☐	*There's no law that says that fathers can't do a workout on Father's Day.*
15 ☐	
16 ☐	*From 1870 to 1900, race-walking was a popular spectator sport. Sports arenas echoed with the cheers of sell-out crowds when heel-and-toers were featured.*
17 ☐	
18 ☐	

June

Walk three or four times a week.

Pace: Pace:

Time: Time:

19 ☐ *Keep an eye out for walkers who look graceful and seem to walk effortlessly. Watch their overall form and learn "by wholes."*

26 ☐

20 ☐

27 ☐ *A secret to improving form is to not try too hard.*

21 ☐

28 ☐

22 ☐ *Today the heavens celebrate by providing the year's maximum daylight hours. We should take full advantage of it. Anyone for a walk?*

29 ☐ *Continue to improve your form. Just a little more polish and you will be modeling a top-of-the-line sports shoe.*

23 ☐

30 ☐

24 ☐ *Start with your own native walking form and improve it gradually. Do not try to adopt a totally new and radically different style. It might work against you.*

25 ☐ *Change your walking route often to ward off boredom.*

July

Pace:

Time:

Walk three or four times a week.

Pace:

Time:

1 ☐	**8** ☐
2 ☐ *Samuel Taylor Coleridge, author of* The Rime of the Ancient Mariner, *walked 10 miles a day.*	**9** ☐
3 ☐	**10** ☐ *Do you live near a beach? That's the place to walk on a hot day. An evening workout there is 10°F cooler than in town.*
4 ☐ *Today you can show your independence of the automobile by walking.*	**11** ☐
5 ☐	**12** ☐
6 ☐	**13** ☐
7 ☐ *If the forecasters have predicted hot weather for today, schedule an early-morning workout.*	**14** ☐ *When you are at the mercy of the sun on a cloudless day, look for a tree-shaded path for your workout. Play it safe in hot weather.*

July

Pace:

Time:

Pace:

Time:

15 ☐	**22** ☐
16 ☐ *Stay well-hydrated on hot days. That means drinking before and after your workout.*	**23** ☐
17 ☐	**24** ☐ *For walking, choose cotton or wool socks. Those made with synthetics don't absorb the perspiration adequately.*
18 ☐ *Select walking shoes with supportive heel counters to stabilize your feet.*	**25** ☐
19 ☐	**26** ☐ *If your workout is long, arrange for a few ounces of fluid every 20 minutes.*
20 ☐ *No matter how good your form has become, walking in the nude can get you arrested, even in hot July.*	**27** ☐
21 ☐	**28** ☐ *While you are arranging for an intraworkout drink, prepare another cupful to pour over your head.*

July

Walk three or four times a week.

Pace:

Pace:

Time:

Time:

29 ☐	**31** ☐ *If the weather is really sweltering, you can do a shorter, slower workout and still hold your head high for having done that much.*
30 ☐	

August

Walk three or four times a week.

Pace:

Pace:

Time:

Time:

1 ☐ *Just think—if you were in Argentina or Australia right now, you'd be freezing to death. Warm is nicer.*	**5** ☐
2 ☐	**6** ☐
3 ☐	**7** ☐ *Pregnant walkers can try full shoe inserts to ease shock and keep feet and legs comfortable.*
4 ☐ *When you buy walking shoes, remember that your feet may swell in the hot weather, so allow for this in the fit.*	**8** ☐

August

Pace:

Pace:

Time:

Time:

9
☐

16 *"Of all exercises, walking is the best." (Thomas Jefferson)*
☐

10 *Warm weather lets you walk in the rain with some pluses. The rain will wash you down and cool you off at the same time.*
☐

17
☐

11
☐

18 *Chances are that you have already gone down a full size in your clothing since July 1.*
☐

12 *The Delaware Indians deeded to William Penn all their land that a man could walk across in 1½ days, expert walkers ticked off an unexpected 66½ miles.*
☐

19
☐

13
☐

20
☐

14
☐

21 *If you walk with a partner, don't let your partner down by skipping a session. Walk three or four times each week without fail.*
☐

15 *If it feels unbearably warm and humid, just think back to that cold snap in February when you had to wear long johns under your warm-up suit.*
☐

22
☐

August

Walk three or four times a week.

Pace:

Pace:

Time:

Time:

23 ☐		**28** ☐	*If you're just out of a sick bed, make your first workout more of a stroll than a workout, just to tone your muscles.*
24 ☐	*If you walk alone, don't let yourself down.*	**29** ☐	
25 ☐		**30** ☐	
26 ☐	*Aerobic (with air) exercise is long, unhurried, endurance activity—continuous, without pause, like walking.*	**31** ☐	*Don't rely on tennis shoes or "sneaker" types of footwear for serious walking. Invest in the right shoes.*
27 ☐			

September

Walk three or four times a week.

Pace:

Pace:

Time:

Time:

1 ☐	*Make walking a part of your life-style and confound the statisticians who are betting that you will drop out of the fitness scene.*	**2** ☐	

September

Walk three or four times a week.

Pace:　　　　　　　　　　　　Pace:

Time:　　　　　　　　　　　　Time:

3 ☐		**10** ☐	
4 ☐	*You are probably so strong by now that walking is no work at all, even on Labor Day.*	**11** ☐	*Maybe walking won't help you to solve the mysteries of the universe, but walking can bring out creativity in your field of expertise.*
5 ☐		**12** ☐	
6 ☐	*Aerobic dance has too much "bounce" for some fat people. Walking is just right for everyone.*	**13** ☐	*Oh, you are an astrophysicist? Well, how about devoting a nice afternoon's walk to formulate a unified field theory?*
7 ☐		**14** ☐	
8 ☐	*Maybe you are strong and steady, but if you have any ideas about entering a marathon soon, remember that 26 miles requires a well-trained walker.*	**15** ☐	*Hippocrates, the father of medicine, wisely counseled that "walking is man's best medicine."*
9 ☐		**16** ☐	

September

Walk three or four times a week.

Pace:

Time:

Pace:

Time:

17 ☐	**24** ☐
18 ☐	*You can perform an important research study today. Compare your present walking ability with your first efforts on the Program. You'll feel gratified.*
25 ☐	*A jogger, passed by a walker, might be very upset.*
19 ☐	**26** ☐
20 ☐	**27** ☐
Office frustrations, an argument at home, car trouble—all depressing and stressful. Your walking workout can help your psyche. Don't skip it when you need it most!	
21 ☐	*"Unhappy businessmen would increase their happiness more by walking 6 miles a day than any conceivable change of philosophy." (philosopher Bertrand Russell)*
28 ☐	
22 ☐	*Be physical.*
29 ☐	*If the jogger clutches his chest in pain, do the kind thing and slow down to see if help is needed.*
23 ☐	**30** ☐

October

Walk three or four times a week.

Pace:

Time:

Pace:

Time:

1 ☐ *At 92, George Howe walked from Savannah, Georgia, to Mobile, Alabama—504 miles in 60 days. Who says you're too old to start a walking program?*

8 ☐ *When your grandchildren arrive by car for a visit tell them about the old days, as you walk with them over the river and through the woods.*

2 ☐

9 ☐

3 ☐

10 ☐ *You can also tell them about your workouts nowadays and try to entice them into forming the walking habit.*

4 ☐

11 ☐

5 ☐ *In October 45°F is not freezing; it's brisk. Walk and enjoy.*

12 ☐

6 ☐

13 ☐

7 ☐ *In October 45°F is the same temperature as 45°F in January. In January you would think of 45°F as balmy.*

14 ☐ *Okay, so Columbus couldn't do much walking on the Atlantic Ocean, but he probably walked around the deck a lot. To celebrate Columbus Day, walk in a parade.*

October

Walk three or four times a week.

Pace:

Time:

Pace:

Time:

15 ☐	**22** *Be active at a pace that is comfortable for you—but be active!* ☐
16 *On Boss's Day, just as on Secretaries Day, a workout is in order a few hours after lunch.* ☐	**23** ☐
17 ☐	**24** *On United Nations Day you can gather walkers of different national ancestry in a walk for peace.* ☐
18 *How about teaching someone who has medical problems how to walk, if the doctor agrees? You just might help to save a life.* ☐	**25** *Take a walk with your mother-in-law on Mother-in-Law's Day. It will surely contribute to family peace.* ☐
19 ☐	**26** ☐
20 ☐	**27** ☐
21 *Twenty-six miles at race pace is more than the human body was meant to bear. Remember Pheidippides.* ☐	**28** ☐

October

Walk three or four times a week.

Pace:

Pace:

Time:

Time:

29 ☐

31 ☐ *Treat yourself this Halloween. The trick is to break your walking record by going just a little farther than usual.*

30 ☐ *How about getting a few people together for a costume walk? Afterward, hot apple cider would warm the ghosts and goblins.*

November

Walk three or four times a week.

Pace:

Pace:

Time:

Time:

1 ☐

5 ☐

2 ☐

6 ☐ *You are lucky to be a walker in touch with your environment. Cyclers go too fast. Runners bounce up and down too much. Walking lets you know where you are.*

3 ☐ *Today you can be an art critic. During your walk through the fall colors, look for shape and size, hue and value, shade, texture, and finish.*

7 ☐

4 ☐

8 ☐ *Some people use their lunch hour for a 4-mile walk.*

November

Walk three or four times a week.

Pace:

Time:

Pace:

Time:

9 ☐ *True, we must learn to walk before we can run. But why run?*	**16** ☐
10 ☐	**17** ☐ *Today may be a good day in your walking career, or it may be only average. Look to weeks and months for progress.*
11 ☐ *If you have completed the first eight weeks of the Walking Program, you will qualify for veteran status in just two more weeks.*	**18** ☐
12 ☐	**19** ☐
13 ☐	**20** ☐ *In cool weather, a good warm-up will increase muscle temperature and that will allow your muscles to work without creaking and groaning.*
14 ☐ *You may be fast enough now to pass some joggers during your workout. Be compassionate; try to say kind things as you go by them.*	**21** ☐
15 ☐	**22** ☐ *"I don't have time to walk" means "Fitness isn't really important to me."*

November

Walk three or four times a week.

Pace:

Pace:

Time:

Time:

23 ☐

27 ☐ *An extra mile today might help your body to deal with that extra helping of pumpkin pie on Thanksgiving.*

24 ☐ *At Thanksgiving time be thankful that walking works as a metabolic exercise.*

28 ☐

25 ☐

29 ☐

26 ☐

30 ☐ *If you have needed pills to calm you down or to rev you up in the past, a consistent walking program may lessen that need. Soon it may be, "good-bye pills."*

December

Walk three or four times a week.

Pace:

Pace:

Time:

Time:

1 ☐ *Walking is enjoyable and that is why we stay with this exercise.*

3 ☐

2 ☐

4 ☐ *Even if it's cold out, don't start out too fast or you will be dawdling at the end of your workout.*

December

Walk three or four times a week.

Pace:

Pace:

Time:

Time:

5 ☐	**12** ☐ *Secret: Walking strengthens the lower back. Even if you have the heart of a race-horse, even if you are as lean as a greyhound—walk for the sake of your back.*
6 ☐	**13** ☐
7 ☐ *Walking is easy on the bones and joints. You can treat your body still more gently by being graceful and fluid in your walking form.*	**14** ☐
8 ☐	**15** ☐ *Good walking form is impor-tant for strengthening the muscles of the back. Walk tall and pull from the heel to power your stride.*
9 ☐ *Walking helps the lungs; any activity that helps the lungs helps the heart.*	**16** ☐
10 ☐ *Enjoy the walker's "high," a euphoria that often comes after a period of sustained exercise.*	**17** ☐
11 ☐	**18** ☐ *Be young of heart—walk briskly.*

December

Walk three or four times a week.

Pace:

Time:

	Pace:
	Time:

19 *Be strong of bones—walk briskly.*
☐

26
☐

20 *Be quick of mind—walk briskly.*
☐

27
☐

21
☐

28
☐

22 *Beat the holiday blues with a cheerful walking workout!*
☐

29
☐

23
☐

30 *Be sure the Walking Program is on your list of New Year's resolutions.*
☐

24 *Yes, there's a lot of walking involved in caroling, but there's also a lot of stopping. Workouts must be uninterrupted.*
☐

31 *If you drink, don't drive, not even after a bracing walk around the block.*
☐

25
☐

Index

Rodale Press, Inc., publishes PREVENTION®, the better health magazine.
For information on how to order your subscription,
write to PREVENTION®, Emmaus, PA 18049.